Back of the Book Summary

A human being's life is *this* moment, right now. The past moments are gone, and the future moments have not yet happened. In this moment, you have either bought or are contemplating buying this book. Something must have caught your eye! I know it's probably the title and rare marbles on the cover that you connect with. This is like no other book you have ever read. It is unique and special. One of a kind.

This is my story about how I reached a point of being sick and tired after thirty-plus years of avoiding, running, and hiding from the sexual abuse I experienced as an eleven-year-old boy. I said to myself over and over for years that it was too hurtful and painful to face head on and heal.

Then, one day, after being exasperated with a completely broken heart and a soul in despair, I heard a still, small voice deep within, calling out to me. That voice called my heart and soul to:

- Confront the darkness.
- Spiritually awaken.
- Heal to the best version of myself.
- Dream and create from purity.

Here is what I know to be true: I hope that by telling my story in an authentic way, it will ignite a passion within you and serve as a catalyst to evoke your own healing process. It is my soul's longing that this inspires and offers hope for healing *your* heart and soul. A new perspective of reaching a place of surrender and vulnerability as human being to move forward in your life.

I discovered something profound on the journey. The weight of bearing an untold story within felt like a brick wall being built on my shoulders each day. Telling my story has released that weight and set me free.

So, my challenge to you right now is to rise above, stand in courage, and transform yourself by telling your story. It is time!

Graphic Design: Praveen Jadhav
Editor: Jeanne Hardt
Internal Design: Jesse Gordon

ISBN (hardcover): 978-1-952884-34-4
ISBN (paperback): 978-1-952884-37-5
ISBN (ebook): 978-1-952884-59-7

Table of Contents

Back of the Book Summary..1

Gratitude and Appreciation Moment...5

The Marble Effect Moment of Dedication...................................7

Introduction...9

Part 1—Confronting a Dark Heart and Soul..............................15

    Chapter 1—What You Resist, Persists..................................17

    Chapter 2—The Abuse: the moment of trauma.......................28

    Chapter 3—The Darkness and Conditioning: the moments
    of pain and suffering and defining a belief system...................35

Part 2—Spiritual Awakening of a Heart and Soul........................49

    Chapter 4—A Powerful, Internal Energy Shift........................51

    Chapter 5—The Epiphany: the moment of awakening..............61

    Chapter 6—The Miracle: the moments of discovering
    a beautiful creation...69

    Chapter 7—The Grassroots: the moment of running home........77

Part 3—Continuous Healing of a Heart and Soul.........................87

    Chapter 8—Patching a Hole in the Heart..............................89

    Chapter 9—The Sun: the moment to rise above......................97

    Chapter 10—The Anchor: the moments to stand up................104

    Chapter 11—The Run: the moments of major transformation
    energy shift..113

Part 4—Creating from a Pure Heart and Soul............................121

    Chapter 12—An Emerging New Purpose and
    Supernatural Calling..123

    Chapter 13—The Revolutionary Dream and Movement:
    the moments to upset the status quo to shine and serve
    humanity's healing...129

    Chapter 14—From my Heart to Your Heart: a moment to
    inspire healing and declare completion................................140

Appendix..147

Gratitude and Appreciation Moment

First and of most importance, I am grateful to God for His unwavering, unconditional grace, mercy, and love.

I am grateful for God's supernatural gift of wisdom, strength, and power that gives me the security and courage deep within to be vulnerable to and for humanity.

I am grateful that I answered God's call to spiritually awaken and heal. God never gave up on me which inspired me to never give up!

I am grateful that I am not just a survivor of abuse, but I am thriving in life now from the abuse.

I am grateful that the abuse has been the greatest teacher in my life to lead me to a space of true authentic deep spiritual connection with God.

I am grateful for my parents Paul and Sue Hill for being a part of God's miraculous plan of creation as He breathed life into me. Additionally, I appreciate their unwavering and unconditional love and support over the last several years as I heal from the abuse. Most importantly, I am grateful for healing, restoration, and forgiveness of our relationship! I love you both with all my heart, forever and always!

I am grateful to my sister, Stephanie Hill Bennett for her unwavering, unconditional support and love all these years. I appreciate all your help with writing this book and offering your passion, gifts, wisdom, and insights. I know this was hard as you and I shed a lot of tears writing this story together. I love you always and forever!

I am grateful for the amazing, elite Co – Active trained and certified human beings that stood for my journey to become a life coach. In that, I received extraordinary coaching to move forward in my life to discover new purpose, values, and the ability to lead myself aligned to God's perfect plan and will.

I am grateful to my life coach, Angela Trainor, for holding an authentic space of true love for my transformation and healing.

I am grateful to have amazing, eagle friends and family that stood by me in the depths of my darkest moments to offer their support, encouragement, and love.

I am grateful to my fellow author and editor, Jeanne Hardt, for her wisdom and expertise in making this book the best version of itself. I appreciate you believing in me and pushing me to be the best author possible.

I am grateful to my graphic design and digital marketing team using their talents to make all of this possible.

I am grateful for you in choosing to read this book and letting me share my heart with you. I long, deep within, for healing in *your* life and stand courageously for that as you read every word on the pages ahead.

Truly, I am just grateful to be alive and breathing today!

The Marble Effect Moment of Dedication

Derrick Hill and Sylvia Stivers, my grandmother
My true love, always and forever. No matter what!

Dear Granny,

I know your spirit and God's presence is with me today as I launch this new book out to the world. Although you are not with our family as of March 28th, 2020 when you went home to Rest in Peace, I feel your spirit with me every day as I live life and serve to make a difference for humanity. What have I been up to since your passing, you might ask? Oh, I grieved your loss for weeks upon weeks, including two weeks after your passing, with the loss of our beloved Goldendoodle dog, Sammee, who you always adored so much. I'm jealous that he's getting to enjoy those yummy homemade biscuits with you now that you always made us! Plus, I have been quarantined in the house with COVID-19 virus, a major pandemic right now. So, with all this extra time on my hands and a challenge from my life coach, I decided to write our book to share my story of healing from childhood sexual abuse. I say "our" book for a reason.

Do you remember when you handed me that jar of marbles when I was five years old? And you sternly and adamantly told me, "Promise me you'll never lose these marbles or give them away, as you're going to need them one day in your life." Well, little did I know that thirty-nine years later, they're on the cover of a book called, *The Marble Effect, A Heart and Soul Healing from Sexual Abuse*. So, I dedicate this book to you as the greatest way I can honor your life and the impact you made on me, our family, and now, humanity!

What I've come to know about your life journey is that you also experienced abuse in your younger years of living. Although we never confirmed it to be sexual in nature by your deafening silence when asked the question, we know that you experienced physical and emotional abuse while growing up in your family. I will just say that for all of us who have been violated sexually, that "silence" resonates deeply, as it is often too painful and dark to talk about, so we bury it.

Whether it happened to you or not, I know this to be true from a still, small voice within, speaking to my heart and soul now. I am called to dedicate this book to you, and God has ordained every moment in our lives together for such a time as this. A time to share my story offering hope, inspiration, and healing for all of humanity.

All my love, always and forever,
Derrick

Introduction

Inspirational Sonnet by Amarjeet Singh – The Resolve
So, from thy grovel, thy pain will spring the
phoenix,
and from thy soil and marshes will spring the
scenic,
for that will of yours remains the strongest of
strong,
it will bury thy pain, it goes out far, wide and long,
and there will be many souls hurt there in the
world,
for many an uncouth have stones so many
hurled,
and many an unwise folk hurt thy fellow people,
so, the pain runs and runs, lasts so deeper,
but that will of yours is stronger than steel,
it will take you beyond the threshold of pain to
peel,
so, make up thy mind, forge the steel in thy veins,
and rise from the ashes and kill thy pains,
for when you command, even the forests shall part,
with the fire in thy eyes and that cold steel in thy
heart!

I want to connect you to this moment for yourself now. A moment where I know there is likely confusion, doubt, and devastation in your heart, soul, and mind from some trauma and abuse—specifically that of sexual nature. It feels as though you're in a constant state of inner turmoil and purgatory. The unthinkable, unfathomable has occurred in your life at some point, and over a period of time; you are assaulted, violated, or trafficked by the sickness and darkness of another human being's perverted, sick will. You feel robbed of all your purity, innocence, youthful, and playfulness as you connect to yourself now.

I want you to close your eyes and imagine yourself rising and springing forth like the phoenix—a magnificent, giant bird that symbolizes your strength, your transformation, and your renewal. You realize something so incredibly powerful happening within you that is beyond your limited human understanding and comprehension. That it is only in the ashes of who we once were where we can rise to become the fire of who we are meant to be! I connect to this in a powerful, magical way, as this has been exactly my experience of healing from the devastation of sexual abuse. I know it's possible for you, too.

I'll be sharing this story about my life in a unique way. It's my own miraculous story told from a space of true, authentic, self-inspired moments.

It encompasses what all great stories have in common: a beginning, middle, and end, but told in present tense. The difference here is the end of the old story of torture from sexual abuse as a child and the beginning of a new story of being able to nurture my wounded, eleven-year-old boy self, now as a middle-aged man. This story shares an end to how I always relate to myself as a wounded heart—an aching, angry, bitter, filled-with-rage heart, as I was blamed and shamed from the sexual abuse I experienced. This abuse and damage to the psyche, the heart, and the soul owned my life for thirty-plus years.

It has created a negative energy inside every cell of my body, including my heart, soul, and mind that connects with everything and everyone in the world. This has often left a dirty, greasy oil or grass stain on anything and anyone around me. The constant stress, anxiety, depression, and anger deep within me was covered up quite well with a fake, pretentious smile. I disguised it well by my supersized, fast-food order of an obnoxious, egotistical pursuit to be the best and drag a trail of pain and hurt for most everything around me.

This was how I connected with the world and humans externally from all the internal hurt, pain, and suffering from the wounded eleven-year-old boy's perspective. Also, I projected all the internal darkness outwardly in relating to people and handling life situations. It felt like a permanent, sealed stamp on the soul, that *this is who I am now* and *how I will be the rest of my life.*

The dream, desire, and purpose to make a difference in the world all feels like a constant pursuit to accumulate more and more stuff with a self-serving attitude and agenda of only what is in it for me. This only numbs the internal pain and agony for just a moment. Always returning are the fixes of material possessions, alcohol, drugs, or sex-highs fade away back to the reality of the internal pain, suffering, and darkness. Breaking the willpower of the ego is a mighty challenge, as it becomes so strong and is often used as a mask to protect, secure, and fight against everyone and everything. You only can see from the lens of all the injustices in your life.

Finally, one day, it occurs: a moment of being brought to your knees, falling face down into the mud, and sliding down that waterslide to the pit of darkness where it feels like there's no way to get out. It's too muddy and slippery. You find yourself completely beyond broken. However, God and the Universal spirit sees differently, as there is a new destiny and dream calling you forth.

I clearly have a path forward now, a new dream and vision of hope, transformation, and rejuvenation to aspire and live as my best version and authentic self—full of love, peace, and joy for all of humanity. I imagine that path of bright light that has been so warming to my heart and soul, as it continues shining its radiant brilliance on this life, and a platform to serve as an opening for your transformation and healing, as well. A platform that gives you the inspiration, space, safety, and courage to tell your story.

I've achieved what I never thought possible. I found my true, authentic self with a clearly defined purpose of being like a marble that shines its radiance and brilliance on humanity's healing.

So, what is this "marble" thing all about, anyway? The marble is a metaphor for what my life journey has been like to this point. So, as I shared in the dedication, my grandmother gave me a jar of marbles when I was five. Soon, you'll connect all the dots in the story some thirty-nine years later as part of my healing and discovering life's purpose again. It's like a supernatural prophetic vision that God placed in her heart to share with me.

Then, there is the toy marble, which comes from broken glass, sand, and among elements that, through a lot of heat and molding, shines bright to fulfill its purpose. Finally, there is the marble that is used in art and architecture that comes from sedimentary rock below earth's crust and goes through a major metamorphosis, which includes an enormous amount of heat and pressure to make it shine its beautiful brilliance. It's no longer sedimentary, it's *metamorphic*. The "Marble" metaphor connection that has had its "Effect" in such a supernatural, powerful way in my transformational journey to heal my heart and soul from sexual abuse.

Through the journey, I've found it magical that when one chooses to free themselves from their attachments in their limited, conditioned thinking and get in a space of creating and imagining what is possible for their life with no limits, then truly the old saying, "the sky's the limit," rings so true for your life.

Now, let's go on a journey together as I tell you my story. I want to show you how to confront the darkness, spiritually awaken, continue to heal, and create from a pure heart and soul again in your life as well. This is a calling for the healing that we all long for—a new, revolutionary movement to create support and community groups of human beings across the world to stand together in a courageous way, with an unwavering support and love for one another through the devastation of trauma and abuse. Quite simply, for you to be seen, heard, and loved for who you truly are!

Part 1
Confronting a Dark Heart and Soul

Here is my little eleven-year-old boy's heart and soul, lying in brokenness and darkness from the trauma of sexual abuse. It feels like a dormant, sedimentary rock beneath the earth's crust, awaiting its discovery and extraction to evolve into a marble for art or architecture. Or it's like the broken glass and sand granules buried in their own darkness, lying in wait for its time to be used to produce a toy marble.

Here is my eleven-year-old self-longing to be seen, heard, and restored back to my true, authentic self again—like that rock, broken glass, and sand longing to shine bright as the marble. Imagine, for a moment, what that rock hiding in place below earth's crust or the piles of broken glass and sand pile, layers on top of layers deep within, must be saying to itself. It feels so heavy, *alone*, not able to see, blinded by darkness and brokenness from the abuse that devastated my pure and innocent pre-teen life year after year. Then there is that moment when a blade cuts through the transformed rock to start the extraction process carefully and meticulously. A coaching process that starts to empower me to start surgically extracting my heart and soul out of darkness and brokenness. This boy was nicknamed "Derrickeboy" early in his childhood by his grandmother.

Chapter 1
What You Resist, Persists

Derrickeboy had a conversation one day with a life coach while sitting on a park bench. This occurred after years and years of living stuck in the past, the abuse, the trauma, and the negative, toxic energy and emotions that continue to persist today.

My curiosity was piqued for the first time after many therapy and counseling sessions over the years, and something that day resonated differently when the coach said to me, "What you resist will always persist in your life." That powerful statement started it all. It's like someone turned on the lights. However, they are on a dimmer switch on low setting. We exchanged contact info, and then, we both got up and left, but both of us knew we had met as part of a destiny calling to heal.

So, I pondered the invitation for a couple of weeks and reached back out to the coach. A two-hour consultation between the coach and me was scheduled to establish the foundation of the relationship. This included defining the roles and responsibilities, setting expectations on how we work together, and establishing what support and accountability looks like. Additionally, we discussed what a safe and courageous space looks like for me and how the coach can create that environment in the relationship. More importantly, we discussed that I would grant power to the relationship, and not to the coach. The coach had no power or authority over me. This is explained as key to create an open, safe, and courageous environment to move forward in the coaching. In the session, the coach and I worked through several exercises connected to life purposes, values, leader within (gut instinct, wisdom), and the saboteurs (negative, critical self-talk). Not a lot opens in the session through the exercises when there is a resistance and hesitancy in letting go of what continues to persist, the trauma and darkness from childhood sexual abuse.

Coach: So, as we start our session today, I want to say a few things to you. First and foremost, you are beautifully courageous. It's an amazing honor to sit here in your presence, and I want you to know this as we get started. I know you don't feel this way right now, so I'll stand and hold this space for you from deep within. I know, without a doubt, that you're naturally resourceful, creative, and whole, just as you are. Also, there's a great strength and power within you to explore and discover your life and path forward from where you are, right now— in this moment. I also want you to know that I'm here with you, no matter what shows up—the good, bad, or ugly—and I am committed to create a delicate, safe space wrapped up in a huge hug of love for you. What do you need from me right now for yourself as we start our time together?

Derrickeboy: I'm having a hard time with all this. I don't know if I can do this.

Coach: What's the hard time?

Derrickeboy: Trusting this. I've lost my ability to trust anything or anyone else. Including trusting myself! It's been a continuous dialogue in my mind of how this happened, how did I not know, *why me*, over and over and over. It somewhat feels like I'm sitting in a dark room with the door closed on my bed, and I've heard a different voice for the first time in years that caught my attention. So, I barely opened the door to peek out to see who it is.

Coach: I'm right here with you, and I'm not going anywhere. What is the different voice?

Derrickeboy: I'm not sure.

Coach: What is it that the voice is saying?

Derrickeboy: "It is time."

Coach: Time for what?

Derrickeboy: I am sick and tired of being in this dark room.

Coach: What does the dark room look like?

Derrickeboy: I don't know. I can't see; everything is black, cold, dark, so it seems like one big struggle to see anything.

Coach: What is the struggle with being in this dark room like now?

As silence fills the session, the coach sees my shoulders slumped, head down, a defeated look with tears starting to well up in my little, blue-grey eyes, and tears flowing down my cheeks.

Coach: It's okay. I'm right here with you. I'm not going anywhere. Let's just sit here now with this. Here's a tissue for you.

There's silence for the next few minutes as the boy sobs with tears of pain and suffering. A deep energy of sorrow and loneliness fills the thick air of the room. Derrickeboy sits there as his tears continue to flow.

Coach: I sensed after the last question that you jumped into a swimming pool, or maybe a sink hole or swamp. What does the pool you just jumped into look like?

Derrickeboy: *Looks up. His tears are flowing, he has a defeated, broken-down posture, as he ponders for a moment.* It feels like a sink hole, like the one on my grandfather's farm that I would ride by so many times on my bike or dirt bike and always wondered what was at the bottom.

Coach: What do you feel is at the bottom of your sink hole right now?

Derrickeboy: It feels so alone, shameful, guilty, embarrassing. Nothing but layer on top of layer of dark dirt falling on me.

Coach: You're so brave right now for sharing that. As you connect with those layers of dirt as your own thoughts and emotions, what are they?

Derrickeboy: No one understands. No one gets it. No one seems to care. It feels like a raging anger and bitterness.

Coach: I want you to know that *I* care. I'm here with you. What is it that no one understands or seems to care about?

Derrickeboy: The abuse, the pain, the suffering, the damage, the wound. That I should just snap out of it and get on with life.

Coach: What does it feel like for you in that no one understands this or cares?

Derrickeboy: It makes me angry, bitter, withdrawn, not to mention how pissed off I feel inside right now.

Coach: I notice your entire body looks tense, you have a stern look on your face, your cheeks are flushed, your fists are clinched tightly—like you're ready to punch something. Is that what you want to do?

Derrickeboy: Yes, I want to punch something.

Coach: Like what?

Derrickeboy: I see me punching myself and everything, *everyone* around me.

Coach: *Silence.* Here's a pillow. *He tosses it to the boy.*

Derrickeboy: What's this for?

Coach: I want you to stand up and place the pillow on the couch. When I say go, start punching that pillow as hard and fast as you can. With each punch, shout out what emotion or thoughts you're punching here now.

Derrickeboy: Really?

Coach: Yes!

Derrickeboy: Okay...

Coach: Ready. Set. Go!

Derrickeboy: *Starts punching the pillow, and after thirty seconds or so, starts naming his emotional hurts as each punch lands on the pillow. The raging anger, bitterness, blame, shame, embarrassment, the abuse, the pain, the suffering, the no-one-understanding or caring!*

Coach: Okay, stop. There's someone you missed here.

Derrickeboy: Who?

Coach: Yourself. You said a while ago you wanted to punch yourself. So, for the sake of spilling blood all over and not inflicting harm on yourself, I want you to punch that pillow and shout your own name with every punch.

Derrickeboy: Okay! *He starts punching the pillow and utters his name softly at first while intensifying into screams over and over and over.*

Coach: *The punches continue to fly.* What is it like to continue beating yourself up?

Derrickeboy: It hurts over and over, repeatedly.

Coach: Okay, that's enough! Catch your breath. As you do, feel the air flow in and out of your lungs. As you inhale, I want to you think of that breath as your strength and exhale your fear and weakness. I also want you to observe what you're thinking and feeling now.

Derrickeboy: Okay... *He does so.*

Coach: So, how do you feel now?

Derrickeboy: I feel better!

Coach: What's better?

Derrickeboy: I'm not as angry.

Coach: It feels like release happened.

Derrickeboy: Oh, yeah!

Coach: What else are you noticing?

Derrickeboy: With every punch, it felt like I released the built-up rage, anger, and bitterness that I was holding in for so long.

Coach: Good. What did you learn here?

Derrickeboy: *Pause... Contemplation...* It's okay to let out your feelings.

Coach: Yes, it is, and what's incredible here is for you being so brave and courageous to go where you've not allowed yourself to go before or in a long time. I knew you could do it. The start of opening yourself up and using your voice to speak what's there for you.

Derrickeboy: I have more to share.

Coach: What is it?

Derrickeboy: I need to tell my story.

Coach: How would telling your story make you feel?

Derrickeboy: *He ponders for a minute.* Free, seen, and heard!

Coach: Okay, that is amazing and wonderful to hear. You *are* amazing and wonderful. So, do you like challenges?

Derrickeboy: Yes!

Coach: All right. Here is my challenge to you. Will you write your story on paper for the world to see?

Derrickeboy: What do you want me to write about?

Coach: I want you to tell your story of the moments of the abuse, the darkness, and the conditioning— meaning how this has impacted your life. Can you do it within the next two weeks?

Derrickeboy: I don't know . . .

Coach: You don't know what?

Derrickeboy: If I can do it in two weeks.

Coach: Then, how much time do you need?

Derrickeboy: A month?

Coach: Okay. How about we target a month, or a month-and-a-half, and I'll schedule weekly sessions to connect and support you along the way?

Derrickeboy: *Smiles.* That will work! There is one more thing.

Coach: What's that?

Derrickeboy: You know I'll have to relive the abuse and all the buried emotions again, right? That scares me.

Coach: I know. And because of that, I promise to wrap you up and hold you with so much love and compassion, and I want you to know that I'm here with you every step of the way. What else do you need from me to support you on this?

Derrickeboy: I need you to encourage me daily and be available to talk to me whenever I need you.

Coach: Absolutely. I'll do that for you. You got this! *Fist bump*. May I hug you? *They hug*. You're so courageous!

As they parted ways, the coach took a moment to internalize the session: *Did I create and hold a safe and courageous space for Derrickeboy? Did I allow him to discover and explore the solution himself? Did I show up as completely present and dance in the moment with him based on what is showing up in the coaching? Did I meet him where he is in the moment and allow him to be in that energy? Did a new awareness and subtle or radical transformation occur?*

The importance of this for the coach and Derrickeboy was to create a safe space, so he could process the energy of all his pent-up emotions in a safe way. This was for Derrickeboy, like punching the pillows in anger, rage, and bitterness and naming these emotions for what they were. When this is done, it allows there to be a shift in energy to whatever emotion needs to process through you, eventually taking you into a healthier energy space.

Life happens to all of us in good, bad, and ugly ways. This could mean a moment, an event, a trauma, a wounding that occurs, and could be sexual, emotional, or physical abuse, a car or some other unfortunate accident, a wartime experience, a loss of a loved one, a job loss, a divorce, a chronic health condition, or a sudden, unexpected disease. You have jumped into this pool of dark energy and find yourself in quite a struggle—quite frankly, in despair and darkness!

- What is the struggle that you cannot let go of?
- What does the pool look like for you?
- What are your thoughts and emotions that you're swimming around in?
- What does a release of this dark, toxic, negative energy look like for you?

• What is it that you continue resisting that persists as that nagging dull headache, day after day?
• What do you want to be different here?
  ◦ How do you see yourself showing up then?
• What story do you need to share to start healing yourself?

Chapter 2
The Abuse: the moment of trauma

In life, there are lots of defining moments that make us or break us. It is in those times that we connect with what we call the good times, the bad times, or the ugly times in our lives. These occur by way of life's key milestones, events, situations, or experiences. In this moment, it's one of those traumatic events that brought forth a realization and awareness of devastation for a human being—specifically, a child. A devastation to the heart and soul that leaves a gaping wound that a metal clamp, stitch, or bandage could never stop from bleeding.

In 1987, there was no sex education class taught at Eastern Elementary school; families rarely talked about such things associated with healthy sexual relationships, or taught what appropriate human behavior is. There were no smartphones with access to the Internet. This kind of stuff was rarely, if at all, talked about during that time. So, how on earth is an eleven-year-old, country boy from Pleasureville, Kentucky to know?

I did feel like something was off, though. I mean, it felt like I lost something, and I felt different. I didn't feel like that innocent, playful, energetic, pure-at-heart little boy anymore. I'd noticed this for several months, but never said anything to anyone, as I had thought it to be just adjusting to a new season of life—being a middle schooler, maturity changes, and such. I was in my seventh-grade year at Henry County Middle School. It was a much different experience than I previously had at Eastern Elementary school. I was officially changing classes with many different teachers and students. Like all middle schools, we switched classes just about every hour with five to ten minutes between them.

I remember the moment I become of aware of the abuse. When I realized that what I had thought was just a normal part of life was otherwise. I became aware that "it" had happened to me. I overheard a conversation in the hallway about someone who had been abused sexually, and now, someone was in a lot of trouble.

In that instant, it all started—the onslaught of confusion, wondering, worry, and panic, along with a great fear inside me. Surely, I hadn't experienced the same thing. *That* couldn't have happened to *me*. I sensed a downward-spiraling vortex of raging thoughts and emotions starting —like firemen sleeping upstairs and being awakened at 3:00 a.m. for a five-alarm fire and sliding down the pole in a mad-dash rush. Except, that slide never landed me on the floor. I only had an infinite wave of emotions spiraling downward. It was like being pulled under an ocean wave.

I can vividly smell his cigarettes, his coffee breath—hear his whispers asking me, "How does that feel?" as he would fondle me and perform oral on me. This happened over and over, several times over a six-month span—as I, a young boy, knew no better. Of course, he wanted the deeds reciprocated.

I recall one occasion where he fondled me and whispered into my ear as we were driving down the road in an old, beat-up, blue, rusty, Chevy truck, "Now, don't you be sticking that thing in a girl. You just might get her pregnant." I didn't understand what that meant at the time, in all my purity and innocence. I didn't know that an incision had been made in my soul, and I had been injected with the darkness and sickness of another human being.

I remember wondering if I should talk to my mom and dad about this. No, why should I, when this surely hadn't happened? I had flashbacks of what he had told me, "Make sure you never tell anyone about this, or you won't be able to come back over and play again or shoot hoops." The questions and bargaining, trying to reach some form of justification, rationalization just kept coming over me in waves while I was pulled further down into the depths of that intense, dark emotion.

Minutes went by, and so did the hours that day, until it was time to go home, and I decided that I'd just remain silent and not say anything. I didn't want to get anyone into trouble. I went back and forth on the swinging roller coaster pirate ship of emotions evening after evening, day after day. The wondering if I should tell my parents was finally behind me by not being allowed to go back over to that trailer again. This due to something else that had happened in our family relationship with this man— like many relationships, we lost touch, due to some form of disagreement or fallout.

That roller coaster of emotions continued day after day, week after week, month after month. I covered it up well, for the most part; however, inside me, it was like a trip on my favorite amusement park ride – a lot of speed, hills, and jarring, along with a stomach constantly in knots of fear, uncertainty, and confusion.

However, one evening, I remember being called into the kitchen from my room, as a couple from the community had come to our house to break the news to my parents—news that would stamp a wound of devastation on my family and our hearts and souls forever.

There was another boy who had filed a complaint with the local law enforcement, accusing the man of sexually abusing him. I instantly went blank and could feel my vision narrowing and my heart drop. My mind traveled back to every single moment, encounter, and emotion of all my time spent with this man and the other teenager who lived with him. Seeing that old, decrepit barn in the corner of the road and the two, yellow and rusty trailers sitting parallel to one another, where he and his mom lived. I saw all the rooms in the trailer, saw all the different spots where "it" had all happened.

I could hear the upset, panic, and every other wave of emotion associated with finding out the devastating news. Then, I started receiving question after question, but I really couldn't comprehend anything. I felt as if I had just passed out.

Bombarded by questions from my parents and from myself, asking what had happened to me. Words couldn't explain what I was feeling right then. All I could do was nod "Yes" to confirm that the abuse happened to me. I couldn't talk or say anything. I sat, staring off into space, numb like lidocaine had been injected into every cell of my body. True shock pumped through every inch of my body. I was filled with a lost feeling, with no ability to feel anything else.

The realization hit me that a man, another human being, had forced his sickness and dark issue upon someone else—a child, at that. No words could describe what was in me at that moment. The script of questions bombarding my child's mind—the confusion, the disbelief that I had been sexually abused by this man for the last six months— rolled in my mind over and over. The questions kept coming, and I had no answers. My lips felt like they'd been glued together, and my tongue felt like it was being suppressed by one of those wooden sticks a doctor uses. Tears welled up in my eyes and flowed down my face like a raging stream after an intense, spring thunderstorm.

One question that kept spinning like a broken record in my mind was, "Why me? Why me? Why me? Why me?" Followed by, "What now? How did this happen? What did I do wrong?" I can still feel and hear my heart racing through all the numbness of my body as I pondered these questions. No answer came. I sobbed uncontrollably as the reality began to set in. That day, I lost my presence and identity as a pure and innocent youthful, charismatic, energetic, rambunctious, mischievous, full-of-life, little boy.

So, how on earth did I connect with this man to begin with?

This all happened when we were working on the farm together—me, him, and the teenager living with him. He would help do projects or jobs with my dad or on my grandfather's farm. He was around our family a lot. He even went to the local Union Baptist Church, where our families both attended. It had seemed like a pure and innocent invitation for me to go over and shoot hoops on the basketball goal attached to their old, decrepit, wooden barn—a typical common sight on the country roads of Kentucky. One never realizes another human being's intention in moments like these—the pretense, the manipulation, the lies, the facade to lure and entice a little boy with one of his favorite things in the world. I would mainly go over to play on the weekends, and it went on for six months.

However, this just didn't start with this man who abused me. It likely began with who abused him, then who abused that person, and so on. This probably went back decades and generations; abuse is a continuous cycle for human beings, even in our world today.

The darkness and sickness of another human being inflicting their unwelcomed, unwanted, perverted will upon you: it comes masked as people you think care about you—such as a parent, grandparent, sibling, step-family members, a minister or priest, a school teacher or administrator, a coach or trainer, organization leaders, or anyone with a position of power or authority over kids they think they can trust.

In life we're presented moments where people, situations, or experiences feel "off" or "unnatural." You see a package sitting alone in a subway system or you experience someone touching or saying something to you in an inappropriate way. The slogans today of "see something, say something"—or in this instance, "experience something, say something"—when something feels "off" was null and voided by my silence and not knowing or understanding all of this. A silence that ends up killing the heart and soul of a pure and innocent child. That silence that leads one on a downward spiral that turns into self-abuse and pushes them even further into the darkness. That evening, when I first realized what happened, I confronted not just the dark of the night, but also the abuse of the silence that had officially landed smack-dab in the middle of my heart and soul.

Then began the internal and external abuse of myself: the trying to process the thoughts and emotions, but not understanding or being equipped to process it in a healthy way. A lack of support, due to the lack of awareness, ability, and knowledge on how to handle such a thing as child sexual abuse in 1987 was the societal reality. So, this all led to me being wounded with raging, toxic, negative emotions buried into the depths of my heart and soul, lying in silence for what seemed like an eternal death sentence.

As my silent abuse presented itself day after day, week after week, year after year, it had to come out somehow. That was where all the darkness manifested itself, until I chose to confront it.

Like the blade cuts into the metamorphic rock in darkness, I know the blade of abuse that cut your heart and soul is felt deep within. I'm certain this has evoked a wave of thoughts, feelings, and emotions for you. I'm here with you, and I hold a tender, delicate space for you as you process this. As you connect with my story of the abuse in your own silence and unique way:

- What are you noticing behind your own silence and possible tears?
- What is your story that needs to be told to the world now?

Chapter 3
The Darkness and Conditioning: the moments of pain and suffering and defining a belief system

Light and darkness have a reciprocal relationship with one another. Before darkness occurs, there is always light, and after darkness, there is always light again. I want to share what the light looks like before the darkness sits in: a little boy's heart and soul spirit of purity, freedom, innocence, imagination, and mischievousness of growing up in Pleasureville, Kentucky on a dairy farm.

I got my first pedal tractor when I was three or four years old, and my legs weren't quite long enough to ride it, yet. However, my parents and grandparents pushed me around, and my big smiles warmed all our hearts and souls. I remember when my grandfather would be out on the farm, using the tractor to farm the land, and I'd imitate whatever he was doing with my pedal tractor, such as square bailing hay or disking tobacco ground. I'd play with my toy trucks, moving dirt from one spot to another and digging trenches to pass time. I once clipped a bunny rabbit's ear with a pair of wire cutters while my dad was busy building rabbit cages, landed myself a spanking, and was sent to my room!

Occasionally, I was known to pick up a few rocks and dirt clods and throw them at whatever presented itself. This often landed me in trouble, as well. I loved skipping rocks across the lake and seeing the ripple effects. I loved running and riding my bike or dirt bike on that quarter-of-a-mile, grass-rock trail with a big, black barn on the way from my parents to my grandparents' house. It was white and had two stories and sat about 600 feet back off the main road. My dog, a boy's best friend, would follow along, tongue hanging out, of course, begging me to stop for some water. I remember all those beautiful sunrises and mornings of eating breakfast on the farm— biscuits with sorghum molasses and lots of butter, gravy, sausage, and bacon. So yummy for the tummy, and its own five-hour energy shot, both from the sunshine and hearty breakfast. I vividly recall helping my grandmother make homemade biscuits and sitting on the counter with her as she said to shake the buttermilk up before pouring it in the flour. I didn't realize the lid was not on, so the kitchen, Granny, and I all took a little bath in buttermilk.

I remember all the trips I took to the garden with my own little pail to gather the harvest of beans, tomatoes, cucumbers, etc. Oh, and the Superman ice cream, swirled with blue, yellow, and red colors from Norm's Grocery market when I'd go to town to get groceries with my grandparents. That connects me to one of my all-time favorite action heroes, Superman. Two scoops, sticky hands, and a satisfied belly full of ice cream later would always bring a sense of contentment and enjoyment as we drove, with Papa speeding over "thrill hill" to give us a good belly flop. This included taking our lives into our own hands, as we'd find ourselves over on the shoulder of the road when he'd look across the truck at the beautiful farmlands, with Granny shouting, "Hold it on the road, Deward!"

Walking in dirt of a farm field ready for crop, or a sports field or court, always touches and warms my All-American heart. As a little boy, I had aspirations and dreams of one day having my own farm or playing in the major-leagues and hitting game-winning shots at the University of Kentucky, my favorite basketball team. Driving tractors by myself at the age of five, while no one called child protective services, my grand-mother and my mom gave my dad and my papa nine shades of hell over that. From that day on, though, I would drive tractors in the fields to pick up bales of hay or sticks of tobacco from our crops. Driving a trac-tor has always been one of my favorite things to do. The old saying, "You can take the boy out of the country, but you can't take the coun-try out of the boy," always rang true for me.

Oh, and I recall all those great family times of Sunday church and fam-ily meals afterward, complete with homemade ice cream from fresh, dairy farm milk. I remember planting and harvesting the garden, throwing dirt clods and rocks, and landing myself into trouble. Every-thing we did provided numerous moments of family connection, love, and joy.

I loved to shoot my BB gun at targets I set up such as metal cans, and on one occasion, at my grandparents' window. I made endless trips on my Honda XR 80 dirt bike around the farm taking in the scenery, pre-tending to be in Motocross racing.

Of course, I must mention the pranks I'd pull on my sister and cousins —like encouraging my sister to step in a crusted-over cow pile with white, strappy sandals as she got a ball out of the cow pasture. That was the day I got my first switching from my grandmother on my little, bare legs! There are so many more memories of extraordinary moments of my being free, pure, innocent, mischievous, and fully connected to life, family, and others, such as friends and community folks.

All those light-filled, beautiful moments suddenly came to a halt, giv-ing way to a darkness from the moments of abuse. It feels like the light, purity, freedom, and innocence I'd enjoyed while running around and playing in the beautiful sunshine was gone.

The darkness of the that first night when I realized I had been sexually abused fell on the countryside land and settled into the heart and soul darkness of that night in my room. I laid in the bed, still devastated, with thoughts racing of what would come next. I could feel the darkness of being alone, withdrawn, and isolated creeping in like a burglar, making his way into the house to steal my heart and soul and destroy me. Silence can be a positive thing when you don't have anything nice to say to someone or to connect you to that still, small voice within; however, it isn't healthy or positive when there are toxic and negative raging, thoughts, emotions, and feelings within, especially after sexual abuse.

The nights, days, months, and years that followed were torturous for me because of all the reprocessing I did of the moments of the abuse, the images, the replaying of the events over and over and over. Like I was trying to find a reason, a justification, an answer to something that did not exist, or at least, did not exist to the mind of an eleven-year-old, even until age of forty-two. I went through 3:00 a.m. sweats, panic attacks, waking up to gripping my soaked sheets on a frequent occurrence. I even started wetting the bed again. All the while, the toy marbles my grandmother had given me were sitting on my shelf, lying in the darkness with me.

The days, weeks, months, and even thirty-plus years that followed the abuse were cold and dark for my parents and me. Surrounding that was confusion, uncertainty, anger, and wondering how best to move forward beyond this devastation. The familiar and comfortable thing for any human is the road of least resistance because silence seems to be less controversial. After all, sweeping it under a rug makes it no longer visible, and stays buried under the fibers of the heart and soul indefinitely. I am certain you can relate to this.

A choice to "sweep it under the rug" and not talk about it was made by my parents and me. This left an ongoing pain inside all of us for decades. It significantly impacted my relationship with my parents for years and years. They still feel the hurt, anger, guilt, blame, and shame upon themselves every single day. It feels like a constant brick wall continuously being built with disconnect, hurt, anger, and unforgiveness deep within. They hurt and beat themselves up for not protecting me, just as I hurt from feeling abandoned and unsupported, at times. It seems like a constant underlying friction and unease within our relationship.

We did explore legal action shortly after discovering what happened. When my father sought the advice of a lawyer, I was adamant I would not testify. What more could a father do? I can tell you what *my* father wanted to do, but that's beside the point. However, I angrily and bitterly did not want it out that I had been abused, especially to my friends and other family members. Charges were not pressed on my behalf, as I had made it clear I didn't want that. The man ended up in prison due to charges brought forth from other boys.

Let's be honest, I grew up in small-town U.S.A., where tractors are as prevalent as cars—we even had our very own Drive Your Tractor to School Day. Everybody knows everybody. I graduated in 1994 from Henry County High School with only ninety kids, so we all knew one another for better or worse, in a sense.

Looking back and being mindful of the cruelty of kids, I didn't want to be different, damaged, or called names, like "gay" or "fag" and God only knows what else. Unfortunately, even today, kids who don't understand what one goes through with abuse will say hurtful things to each other. Teenagers can be brutal on kids, not even knowing the damage that has been done and continues to be done to one's soul. I didn't want to be labeled as different or *weird*. This leaves another mark on your psyche and how you see yourself as well. So, to avoid all of that, I adamantly did not want it out. I found in life that what one says about you, or you say about yourself, has a great power over you and leaves a positive or negative footprint on your heart and soul.

Pain and suffering through life experience and specific moments is inevitable. You're going to get hurt in life, whether it be physically, emotionally, or spiritually. In those hurts or wounds, you might say painful events happen to us, and then, comes the suffering that lingers on in life. Some is temporary, like a nagging toothache, and some suffering lingers on for years and years—sometimes, forever if never dealt with. For example, you might fall and break an ankle. Immediately, you're going to feel instantaneous pain that goes away once you get the right treatment and medications to treat the pain. Then, the suffering sets in with the healing and rehabbing, while you're on crutches trying to maneuver around and live life and fulfill your responsibilities.

The physical moments of temporary pain and suffering for me have consisted of numerous events. I fell out of a sliding glass door when I was two years old and hit my forehead on a brick. I required stitches. I guess my parents had been ignoring me or something! I turned my dirt bike over and caught my leg under the muffler, resulting in a third-degree burn and extensive medical treatment. Then, there was the line drive hit off a baseball bat directly to the face when I was about twelve-years old, pitching in the All-Stars, and it instantly knocked me out cold. I had a concussion and a swollen face with no broken bones. I'm lucky it didn't kill me. I also had a football injury that consisted of fractured ribs and a concussion, and sixteen stitches in my chin after another brutal hit by two defensive linemen. My list of injuries can go on to the current day. In those moments, the pain and suffering are immediate, temporary, and forgotten quickly; they become a distant memory, with no lingering suffering. You see, these are all externally painful moments and easier to recover from quickly.

I have also experienced emotional and spiritual moments of pain on numerous occasions. The first major moment was the sexual abuse. I was also made fun of, bullied, or ignored at school by kids several times, all the way from elementary school to high school. For example, I remember being called "gay" or "weird" on many occasions on the bus and playground, and I internalized those harsh words into my heart and soul. It started affecting how I saw and related to myself and others in the world around me. Whether it was their own jealously or issues, I allowed that to influence me greatly, which created a belief system for how I see and feel about myself. It destroyed my confidence and disconnected me from my true self.

I grew up in a strong, Baptist family, where we attended church each Sunday in our Sunday best. You would find my grandparents at the kitchen table every morning at 5:30 a.m., reading their Bible before their day on the farm started. Despite this, I was angry at God. How could He have let this happen and why? Why could He not make the darkness just stop?

Despite my parents trying to seek legal action, I felt devoid of support and protection, which followed me to adulthood. I knew they weren't to blame, but it ate at me— how could they not have seen? How come they never taught me that if someone did sexual things to me at that age, it was wrong?

Those feelings followed me, even after I had my first child at twenty-eight years old. Right after my son was born, I remember having a heated argument over a coat that Mom had given me that my sister thought had been my grandfather's. I peeled out of their long driveway and stopped at the end to throw out the baby book and clothes that Mom had bought my son. I was so angry that I didn't want *anything* from them. I just felt so unsupported.

From that point on, it all turned into one, hellacious life struggle, like a battlefield of the mind, heart, and soul. There were continuous, ongoing moments of pain and suffering through various events and phases in my life. However, one thing I held onto that seemed to alleviate the pain and suffering through my teenage years and on into becoming a young adult was sports—baseball, basketball, and football in middle and high school. It gave me an outlet where I could focus on something else to temporarily relieve the pain.

You get acclimated to winning and losing. There's nothing wrong with winning in life; however, what the motive is behind it means everything. The competition, the drive to win at all costs and prove myself over and over, seemed to be the thing that helped me feel better and soothe my heart and soul—not realizing all that was doing was creating a monster of an ego that later turned into a have more, be more, at any costs attitude. Throughout high school, college, finding jobs, starting a family, and building relationships with people in the community and church, it was all a continuous struggle; I was constantly trying to prove and win, and I was leaving a trail of bodies along the way.

This is how I treated people when I was only acting and speaking out of the rage, anger, bitterness, withdrawal, and isolation. It was all a protective mechanism to cover up the suffering, as I was often just staring off into space, unable to express or feel any kind of emotion.

As the years progressed into my twenties and thirties, more pressures in life built with establishing a career in healthcare and information technology, getting married at twenty-three-years old, starting a family with our two boys—Landon and Chandler—at twenty-eight. Not to mention, the pursuit of materialism—bigger and better houses, big businesses, nice cars, high-quality clothes, high-end technology and gadgets, and so on. I was living in this fake news story in my mind that these things were what truly created happiness, fulfillment, and contentment. I was trying to find contentment in all these things, and they became my true purpose and value. Like, this is who I was or something!

Trust is as delicate and precious as the sedimentary rock laying below earth's crust. It is delicate and must remain intact and not be crushed to end up producing marble. In human relationships, we want to trust and give our trust to others. It can take days, months, or even years to build trust with someone, but that can be shattered in a split second—like a sudden, tragic loss of life in an accident.

I quickly lost faith and trust in all human beings, but more importantly, I lost the ability to trust myself. This led to dark feelings of insecurity, inadequacy, guilt, blame, and shame. It manifested as anger and bitterness. I often covered this up with a mask of arrogance and pride. So, when an opposition or challenge came, I used this energy state to leave a trail of negativity, obnoxiousness, and prideful words and actions; plus, I cut people off and out of my life immediately.

Being physically present but not being emotionally connected to myself or anything else felt like black copy paper being fed through a photocopy machine day after day. As the light from the machine tried to scan the original copy, there was nothing to print. Dark letters on dark photocopy paper only shows a dark-conditioned heart and soul.

Numbness from the pain and how that conditions us shows up in a lot of different ways for people. Some find relief by acting out what is done to them on another; some go into angry rages to the point of violence and harming others, but most become obnoxious and egotistical and begin using substance abuse, pornography, or sexual self-abuse with many different partners, and so forth. It seems like they are in a constant pursuit of the love they only think they deserve. This is what the darkness from abuse does to the human spirit.

For me, this is exactly what my experiences were: pornography, substance abuse – mainly alcohol, but some drugs, like THC—obnoxious ego, selfish actions and behaviors, including angry outbursts of rage, and using women as an object of sex to instantaneously gratify my selfish, dark desires. Thank God I never acted out my own sexual abuse on someone else. The abuse I projected on others was always verbal and physical in nature, which was damaging in its own right. That damage to other human beings, like verbal negativity toward my kids, I've had to process and reconcile within myself to forgive, heal, and restore relationships.

The post traumatic effects on a heart and soul from abuse is real and lingers like a nagging toothache over the course of one's life. I was never officially diagnosed by therapists or counselors as having Post Traumatic Stress Disorder (PTSD) from the abuse, but all those side effects influenced my energy state and how I appeared to others. I did try counseling a few times when I was going through some tough times, like almost divorcing at years five and twelve. It helped a little, but it never offered much in the way of deep heart-and-soul level transformations, which I'll describe in later chapters in this book. Whether I was awake or asleep, I always felt a zinging energy of anxiety and nervousness embedded in every cell of my body, which created an underlying blockage of flow. I would have shaky hands, sweaty palms, and cold, wakeup-sweats once the alcohol would wear off.

Life by my mid-to-late thirties felt like I was on one of my favorite rides at Holiday World—the Zinga Water ride. It's a vortex slide that swirls you downward with raging water and shoots you out at the end of the ride. I felt like my life at that time was like a storm crate drain cover was blocking that exit chute, and I was stuck in the chute while the water kept rushing and pounding my body. This left me feeling exhausted, overwhelmed, and drowned. It weighed on me physically and mentally over time, leading to even more of a downward spiral of mental health challenges and behaviors—including a heart and soul that felt bankrupt and empty. Plus, my abuse of alcohol only intensified from my early thirties until I hit rock bottom in the spring of 2018 at forty-two-years old.

I often internally felt as though I was standing on the Golden Gate bridge in San Francisco, staring at Alcatraz in the middle of the water. I felt like I was on a daily boat ride to my own prison cell. I would want to lock myself up for the day and free myself at night with my numbing substance of choice.

As I continued to live with this notion of "fake it until you make it" over the years, I defined a belief system. What one hears, says, or thinks of themselves, they believe—whether it's good or bad.

As I connected with myself through pictures or by looking in the mirror each day, it felt like I was the only one who could see the darkness, the pain, and the suffering I had within me. This was all due to the soul-killer of "silence" deep inside me. Over time, this formed a negative belief system about how I saw myself and the world, as well as other human beings. Only the eyes of the abused connect with the eyes of the abused, and "just know" the devastating hurt and pain that lies at the core heart and soul of us.

There were also other factors that conditioned me to form these beliefs. The influences of many different religious views – Baptist, Christian, Non-Denominational, and Denominational—the different teachings about judgement, and the hypocrisy that tends to turn away the broken and bleeding hearts and souls looking for relief. The same can be said about social classes, races, and ethnicities in America and being put into boxes, labeled, and shipped down the road to the destination of "The Rich," "The Middle Class," or "The Poor."

The continuous labels and our biases, prejudices, and perspectives toward one another, plus the federal and state governments, educational systems, and cultural conditioning from family upbringings, all add to the formation of a belief system. All these things managed to push their own agendas and tell me who I was, what I could have, and how I was to live my life.

While this has some positive aspects— such as morals, ethics, and standards— it most often impacted my individuality and connection to my true, authentic self. This robbed me of my freedom and independence and often blocked discovering and exploring my gifts, talents, passions, and creativity. All this brought me to a breaking point, one which I will never forget.

As I sat on the park bench on a number of occasions in April and May of 2018 at Waterfront Park in downtown Louisville after a day of working for a healthcare IT employer, I was sitting in a puddle of an eleven-year-old boy's tears of sorrow at the age of forty-two. This happened day after day for a couple of months— whether I was on the park bench, sitting in the car, or driving down the street. Broken, in despair, and in the middle of a family crisis and a marriage separation that was ultimately heading for divorce after twenty years together. I felt so alone, withdrawn, isolated, bitterly angry, scared, and insecure.

A little boy's abused, dark heart and soul was now in a grown man, and the silence continued to kill me. My life had completely fallen apart, and I was at the bottom of a dark, slimy sinkhole, with layer on top of layer of what felt like dirt covering me. I didn't feel this way because of the family crisis or the divorce, but I had felt this way ever since the abuse and the emotional conditioning I had experienced afterward.

Heat and pressure from everyone around us can shape and mold us to become what we are *not* meant to be and can define who we think we are. That same heat and pressure are how marble is used to make a toy or art, because it must be refined through its own process of evolution and metamorphosis. I've discovered through life's journey, that one must experience that same transformation to arrive in a new place of self-awareness and awakening.

YOUR
Marble
EFFECT MOMENT

Like the marble's connection to the darkness as sedimentary rock, the broken glass and sand granules lying in a pile, and like all my moments of pain, suffering, and darkness I just shared, you must also be experiencing something similar.

- What is the pain, suffering, and darkness look like for you?
- How has this impacted your life?

Part 2
Spiritual Awakening of a Heart and Soul

The heart and soul of Derrickeboy reached a key pivotal moment in life. It was a lot like walking a path and reaching a crossroads in the road, when there came a calling by some higher power, like God. It was a crossroads where—whether he realized it or not—presented him the opportunity to choose. It was a choice that would either move him forward or set him even further back—which meant, quite simply, to live or die. Should he take the path that would start the process of going forward to the light or slide down further into the hole?

In a sense, it was a lot like marble's path into its beauty as it continues to lie in darkness as sedimentary rock, fine sand granules, or a pile of broken glass, waiting to be made new, whole, and complete. Suddenly, one day, it feels all the movement—movements made above or around it that is about to push the dirt, sand, or glass to make its choice to take one step closer to the light: a choice that will lead it to its shining brilliance. Or, if it does nothing, it will remain in darkness.

Mining the marble for art and architecture involves a lengthy, quarrying process. It entails digging the dirt away from the desired rock while establishing roads and tunnels to make its access more efficient. Each cut must be meticulously overseen to ensure its purity and integrity. It all starts with a "bench wall," where that cut is made as the dynamite blasts loosen the rocks for separation. The additional cuts create perfect, individual, uniform blocks. This whole process is a lot like Derrickeboy's transformation and coaching relationship. A relationship where the coach serves as an expert, trained-and-certified guide to connect him to a new choice, commitment, and action path forward—a new way of being discovered from the magic in the relationship.

Chapter 4
A Powerful, Internal Energy Shift

Coach: Welcome back to our time together. I'm glad you made the decision to come. I just want to say what an honor it is to have supported you over the last month, daily and weekly, as you wrote your story of the abuse and darkness, and the traumatic impact that it has had on you. You're an amazing boy, so courageous as you step into this extremely uncomfortable space. I know it's hard, but you're doing it! So, what did you learn from that writing exercise of telling your story?

A long pause.

Derrickeboy: I don't know for sure.

Coach: What *do* you know for sure right now?

Derrickeboy: I guess... I wrote my story.

Coach: You guess, or you did?

Derrickeboy: I did.

Coach: What's opening up for you from writing it?

Derrickeboy: *Long pause.* That I can tell my story, but it still hurts deeply.

Coach: I know... I can see the sadness on your face. Let's do this. I want you to take a couple of deep breaths for me right now and just feel the air flow into your nostrils, down into your lungs, and back out through your nose.

Derrickboy: Okay... *Takes five, semi-deep breaths.*

Coach: What's do you feel now?

Derrickboy: Sad and hurt.

Coach: Where do you feel the hurt?

Derrickboy: My heart aches... *The tears start welling up in his eyes...*

Coach: I'm here with you, and I'm not going anywhere. I see tears and sadness on your face. What's behind the tears?

Derrickboy: There's a deep hole.

Coach: The sink hole on your grandfather's farm?

Derrickboy: No.

Coach: What's the hole? Here's a tissue... Take your time to be where you are...

Silence and pondering set in for the next few minutes.

Derrickboy: It's in my heart.

Coach: The hole is in your heart?

Derrickeboy: Yes.

Coach: I got this visual of a bow and arrow aimed right for your heart, and it shot the hole there. What do you see?

Derrickeboy: It feels like that.

Coach: I sense it's from writing and telling your story, and it's like a bandage has been ripped off the wound. What do *you* sense?

Derrickeboy: It's gushing...

Pause.

Coach: Say more?

Derrickeboy: It's like gushing out all this *stuff*.

Coach: What's the stuff?

Derrickeboy: The anger and hurt from the abuse.

Coach: What is truly behind this anger and hurt?

Derrickeboy: The guilt, the shame, the blame.

Coach: What else?

Derrickeboy: That's all.

Coach: As all that gushes out of your heart, what do you think will stop the gushing?

Derrickeboy: I don't know...

Coach: Let's play a little game right now. How does that sound?

Derrickeboy: A game of what?

Coach: Hoops.

Derrickeboy: I don't know...That's how the abuse all started to begin with!

Coach: I see. So, what is the hesitation here for you now?

Derrickeboy: I don't want it to happen again.

Coach: Remember when we formed our relationship, that only you can grant that power to the relationship?

Derrickeboy: Yes.

Coach: Remember that discussion about my commitment to create a safe and courageous space for you?

Derrickeboy: Yes.

Coach: It's up to you whether or not you want to go outside. I want to remind you of my commitment and responsibility here, so I assure you, you're not going to be taken advantage of again. So . . . what would you like to do here *now*?

The boy's face lights up with a smile...

Derrickeboy: Let's go!

Coach: What is the smile about?

Derrickeboy: Playing basketball is one of my favorite things to do.

Coach: What is it you like best about playing basketball?

Derrickeboy: I love to pretend I'm playing for UK in a championship game and hitting the game-winning shots.

Coach: Wow, sounds like you're quite the player on that court, to be hitting game-winning shots.

Derrickeboy: I love being the hero, the go-to person in the game. Then, being the center of the celebration and getting tackled on the court, with streamers flowing from the rafters.

Coach: You *are* a hero, and I see quite the player here. What is it like to be celebrated and tackled on the court?

Derrickeboy: Oh, it's a great feeling!

Coach: What does it feel like?

Derrickeboy: Power, strength, and courage!

Coach: What else?

Derrickeboy: That's it.

Coach: You mentioned this word "love" and how you *love* to play the game. How are they connected?

Derrickboy: In the zone I feel good and full of energy. Playing the game feels natural.

Coach: Wow, that's amazing! I see that you're *currently* in the zone, and I hear something different in you. Who are you, right now, as you play this game on the court?

Derrickboy: I'm courageous enough to take the winning shot, powerful and strong enough to play the game, and excited enough to love to play the game. It's fun!

Coach: Let's go on a little imaginary journey right now in this space you're in. Lay the ball down, and imagine you're playing this same game on this court. However, the game isn't about you hitting the game-winning shot, this is about you healing from the abuse, darkness, and impact on you. What does the game-winning shot look like now?

Silence for a couple of minutes.

Derrickboy: I want to feel like me again, like that boy full of life—pure, innocent, and playful.

Coach: Let's pick the ball back up. When you're ready to take the shot to create what you want here, go ahead and let it fly.

Derrickboy: Okay, give me a minute.

Coach: Take your time.

Derrickboy: I shot the ball and *swoosh*, I hit it!

Coach: A lot like hitting that shot, it's possible that you just hit the game-winning shot for yourself! How do you see yourself moving forward here, then?

Derrickeboy: It's time to play the game.

Coach: You're so amazingly courageous, playful, strong, and powerful. I have a request for you. Will you start the process of patching the hole in your heart by making a list of what you want to create to move you forward and heal? You can say *yes, no,* or *another offer.*

Derrickeboy: Another offer.

Coach: What do you want?

Derrickeboy: I want you to help me work on my list and filling that hole back up in my heart each day.

Coach: You got it! How about we schedule thirty minutes a day for the next couple of weeks until our next session?

Derrickeboy: That sounds good!

Coach: I have another request. Remember I asked you to take some breaths earlier in our session?

Derrickeboy: Yes.

Coach: What happens when you breath in and out like that?

Derrickeboy: I feel more focused. *Calmer.*

Coach: Great, then will you practice breathing in and out at least for two to three minutes to start each morning and evening, and as needed when you start feeling upset or stressed out?

Derrickeboy: I really liked that, so yes, I'll do that.

Coach: There's one more thing I want to ask of you.

Derrickeboy: What?

Coach: Will you start saying some positive things to yourself after your breathing session?

Derrickeboy: Like what?

Coach: I am courageous. I am energetic. I am strong. I love being playful. I am healing!

Derrickeboy: All right. Plus, I want to write it on a card or something and carry those with me each day.

Coach: How about using one of those little, over-the-door, indoor basketball sets? You can get a foam basketball and write those statements on it.

Derrickeboy: Yeah! That way, when I shoot them, I'll have a reminder, and I can also carry that foam ball in my backpack.

Coach: That's awesome! You're so creative.

As the session ended, the coach realized a shift had happened for Derrickeboy. A shift that had brought him into a new awareness, perspective, and energy. It was the start of a major healing and transformation.

Every beautiful thing that is created starts from somewhere or something, just like the marbles Derrickeboy received at five years old.

As the coach checked in with his connection to the principles of coaching, he asked himself some questions: *Did I utilize the process aspect of coaching, where I meet Derrickeboy in his current energy state and let him be there as he works through it? When a shift in energy occurs, did I continue to build further resonance? Did I use a balanced approach in shifting the perspective of Derrickeboy, as he continued to be stuck in an internal struggle? Did I bring him to a new, resonant choice, commitment, and a forward path of action? Did I offer him requests to facilitate further life experiments to continue the path of healing and new discovery in life?*

As you connect with the coaching session requests the coach asked of Derrickeboy, there are a couple of questions for you:

• What will it take to start patching the hole in your heart and soul?
• Take a deep breath. Let's imagine it as a beam of light, as you count to four on the inhale. Then, let's imagine it as the darkness for a count of six on the exhale. Do this for a couple of minutes. What are you noticing?
• Who are you anyway? I am [fill it in]!

Chapter 5
The Epiphany: the moment of awakening

As I sit in silence at the bottom of the ocean, I take in all the senses connected to a soul's whisper and longing to just be still. It is a moment to just trust myself in a restful presence of blissful consciousness— to respond to the supernatural call to be surrendered, vulnerable, and full of peace and love. For this is what I am and what all human beings long for. I feel the intense sensations of elation and exuberance from deep within. It's incomprehensible and unexplainable how this happens. I also have a deep gratitude for the choice I was given to reclaim my power back over my life and the gift of meditation I have given myself.

It all started the morning of May 29th, 2018. As I was waking up, I was exhausted, broken, desperate, dark, chaotic, turmoiled, and confused. Plus, I still didn't want to accept the sexual abuse and the fact that my family was about to be broken apart, with divorce looming on the horizon in the months ahead.

I noticed the bottle-and-a-half of wine I had drunk the night before had worn off, and the intense anxiety and raging thoughts were once again present after only three hours of sleep. The numbness was gone, and I was left wondering how I could go through another day like this. As I recall that moment, I sit now with tears in my eyes and a cold chill moving through my body.

I got myself semi-together to head into work, but there was something different. Something stirred deep within me as I stirred my coffee. I hurried out the door, as I was already late, and rushed into work as usual, dismissing what was brewing within.

Later that morning, around 11:30 a.m., I was in a conversation with a couple of close friends and confidants after a meeting. They remarked about my exhaustion and expressed their concerns over the anxiety and fear radiating out of my body, as I sat slumped in the chair, defeated. My voice was crackling with doubt, even raising in tone at times in despair. They knew all about my struggles. But this moment was different: they could sense I had reached a breaking point, a depth of brokenness that now threatened my well-being. Their space, support, and encouragement seemed to fall deafly into my consciousness. It felt like someone was talk-ing with a cloth over the speaker, and all I could hear were muffled sounds, until one particular point in the conversation.

They acknowledged and championed me as a human being and the leader that they had witnessed and known me to be over the years. They said, "We believe in you as a leader who never gives up." Then, they asked a powerful question that touched deeply into my soul, "What does it look like for you to take back your power over all of this?"

I sat, silently contemplating that question, not knowing the answer. However, I could feel a little spark of light, like a match first touching the wick of a firecracker for the first time, setting it afire for an eruption and explosion of light.

As I sat there in silence, the tears began to flow. I realized something I hadn't connected with in a long time—or quite possibly, *ever*, in my life. I began to connect back to something that brought forth these defining words, "I am sick and tired, sick and tired, sick and tired." Did I mention how sick and tired I was of giving all this nonsense full con-trol and power over my life? Giving over my God-created-and-ordained supernatural power, greatness, and wisdom within to everything and everyone else?

I wanted to be over and done with it! They could trample, stomp, and disregard all of it as garbage being tossed in a dumpster, then take every bit of it to the landfill to rot away!

As I left the room, time seemed slower. I was absorbed and distracted as I processed what had just happened. It felt like the outer edges of a forceful, category-five hurricane were swirling around and around inside me.

It was around lunch and time for my workout at the fitness center. I was in a complete blackout the whole journey down the twenty-two flights of the building and out the side door about half-a-mile to the gym. Then, it happened: I was walking under the second street bridge in downtown Louisville after going through the KFC Yum center. As I passed the shadow of the bridge into the clear, open path of bright sunshine beaming down on the street, I felt it! I looked up, and the blinding rays of the sun instantly sent a warm, tingling sensation throughout my entire body.

I closed my eyes and kept my face to the warmth. An incredible shift happened and I sensed a deep, soul-level whisper of, "I am here. It's time to come home and reclaim your self-power and strength that is already within you!" It was a lot like that moment when Saul, on the road to Damascus, was touched and moved by the higher power of God and the Spirit whispering in *his* ear. That voice said to me, "Paul Derrick, Paul Derrick, why do you continue to persecute Me and yourself?"

I simply stood there, soaking in that moment of soul nourishment. It was as though I was a blooming flower, feeling the rays of sunshine that were penetrating down into the core of the roots, surrounded with just the right amount of moisture to spur on growth. I immediately realized that one, fine, spring day in May, with a clear, blue, spacious sky, was not a cloudy one. Literally and figuratively. A gentle soft and subtle wind was grazing my skin. The radiant, beaming rays of sunlight were filling my soul with warmth, peace, strength, love, joy, abundance, and a sense of destiny calling me to something new.

After several minutes of standing in the sunshine and resting here now in this deep, supernatural, spiritual connection, I sensed a strong calling and nurturing. I raised my hands and head to the sky to be blinded by the light again. Once I resumed walking, there was a different feeling: a confident swagger, with my head up high, shoulders back with assurance, and a sense that deep within, all was well and would be okay. This amazing shift of the body brought a new energy of swag and confidence, an optimism and deep-knowing belief within that totally shifted how I'd start showing up to others.

Bursting with a new energy, I went on about my day with an awesome workout. There was a new presence deep within me and clarity bubbling like a newly opened bottle of champagne. It had actually always been there, but I'd just rediscovered it through an appointment with the supernatural, divine intervention by the hands of the Almighty. This was only after being in such a broken, rock-bottom barrel of emptiness and a state of complete darkness. It was like a light switch had been turned on in a dark room, and the energy of the light was shining bright enough to show me the exact path to walk on. I realized in the moment that the time had come to take myself to a place I'd never dreamt possible, given the dark, internal state within that had persisted for so many years.

I began to focus on myself and my growth through new disciplines to keep me in this positive space and awareness present within. It was a like a tug-of-war struggle, an outright battle in the spiritual universe be-tween the polarities of darkness and light, good and evil. Let the spiritual warfare begin. I knew I needed to quickly pivot my mind and start retraining and reconditioning it. As one thinks, so shall they be! I have found the mind to be a powerful instrument, that, if left unattended, unnurtured, and not exercised, leads one down paths of emotional turmoil. That brings forth anxiety, depression, fear, despair, hopelessness, and unauthentic connection and expression.

When I met *me* in this powerful, transformative moment, I quickly realized that the story and all the attachment to playing a role wasn't at all who I was. I wasn't all the things I'd told myself that I am. I am not abused. I am not a slave. I am not in a prison. I am not broken. I am not defeated. I am not wounded forever. I am *not* a victim.

I discovered that I must immediately turn around my mind from all my negative thoughts. The mind is like the waves— either choppy or raging, no matter if it's a calm or stormy day. There's always a constant flood of thoughts coming and going, day and night. These thoughts dictate the energy and emotional states of the body at any given point in time. So, for me to break this pattern of negative, critical, and judgmental thinking of myself, others, and everything else around me, I had to create a new discipline to move forward.

I investigated different ways to meditate and calm the mind. Over the course of time, I learned how to use meditation as a tool and technique to create positive thinking habits. In certain instances, even in the Bible there are passages about the power of meditating on His Word. I landed on a meditation practice for its simple, easy, and effortless way of feeding the mind daily. While silence often kills your soul, its power can also heal you. What food is for the body to give us energy and sustained living, meditation practice is to the mind. And since most of us don't care to go a day without eating, meditation needs to be done consistently, such as twice a day for me. So, I choose to give myself the first gift that aligned with this new perspective, by focusing on and becoming the best version of myself to give out to the world.

After this powerful moment of awakening and the renewal of hope and energy from that moment, I left work that evening and signed up for the meditation training with a local instructor near me. Looking back now, I realize that after completing the training, it was the first and best Father's Day gift I've ever given myself. I knew I had to do something that would empower me to arrive at being a connected and healthy man. I wanted to be a positive example and dad to my two boys, and sharing that I was doing this training over Father's Day weekend sent a strong message: Dad is now choosing to take a stand for his life and focus on becoming the best father and human being possible.

However, since I had to wait for fifteen days before the class started, I had to do something immediately to start feeding myself positivity and retraining my mind. I had a great support system of friends at work who offered a lot of great insights and shared various tools and resources.

I recall listening to numerous motivational videos by Fearless Soul and other motivational, pastoral speakers, such as T.D. Jakes, Joel Osteen, Les Brown, Zig Ziglar, and so on. I did this a number of times throughout the day, and the messages began to resonate deeply within me. This created an opportunity for me to start connecting with a new message of purpose, values, energy, and power within. I started reflecting and journaling as I found things nourishing. I listened to video after video, well over ten times a day. Retraining my mind and feeding it positivity had to be a constant, focused discipline.

What I didn't realize at the time is what I call the "resonance of transcending," which to me is making a conscious choice to go beyond the normal, rise and climb higher, and be extraordinary by breaking the limited, ordinary, mediocre ways of thinking. I realized that to accomplish something, I had to expect something of myself, which is a fundamental shift from me expecting something to happen externally. It must all start within me first.

I recall listening to several free motivational videos from Fearless Soul, and there was one that started the whole connection to me affirming myself in a positive way. This isn't about stating it and knowing it from an intellectual standpoint, but this is about stating an affirmation about myself and "feeling" that affirmation with a new energy inside—like telling myself, "I am powerful. I am courageous. I am well. I am healthy. I am love. I am peace. I am joy."

As I found myself connecting with those statements, I began to feel what I was saying about myself, which created a positive, healthy connection to seeing and holding myself differently. One powerful statement I remember saying, "It's my time, and I'm all about focusing solely on me and being the best version of myself to give out to the world, family, and community."

Then, another powerful moment happened when I stepped into my first training session for meditation practice. I'll never forget the apprehension and nervousness I had felt. I knew I couldn't just feed my mind motivation, I had to be able to rest my mind and calm it down, so I could reconnect the heart and soul, as well—something I'd never been successful at for years, while living in the darkness from the post-traumatic stress disorder.

YOUR *Marble* EFFECT MOMENT

I'm curious about the moment you felt so sick and tired of how life was going for you. You sense something stirring within. Then, in a moment, you finally realize something magical and mysterious for yourself!

- What does your epiphany moment look like for you?
    - Quite possibly, how is ignoring it serving you?
- As a man or woman thinketh about themselves, so shall they be! If you want to start feeling differently about yourself, then what do you need to start saying about yourself now?

Chapter 6

The Miracle: the moments of discovering a beautiful creation

The meditation training lasted over four days, and I noticed an instant connection again to a "still, small voice" deep within me—a whispering from "I AM" to let it go, a stillness to just know that I was in the supernatural realm with God. As I settled into the moments of meditation practice twice a day thereon, morning and evening for twenty minutes each session, I noticed something immediately shift: a supernatural, blissful connection to nothing but a cool and calm feeling in the depths of who I was, my spirit. My spirit became my sixth sense once I regained all five of my senses.

This moment is not about a religion, a pastor, or any other man or woman connecting you to the Higher Power, because that is not possible. This was between God and me only. A true connection to that still, small voice deep within was planted there the day I was conceived in my mother's womb. A day when God created and saw me as a beautiful masterpiece and called me to do great things for Him. That great, supernatural power and strength was given to all of us to be able to withstand this life on earth. Quite simply, a moment to be still and just know God's powerful presence deep within.

An authentic heart and soul connection mean the mind must be out of the way and not driving the bus anymore. The bus—your mind—has to be sitting still. It's like I'm resting at the bottom of the ocean, where no matter how rough and choppy the waves are on the surface, it's always calm and cool. Our minds are always so active and bombarding us with obsessive thinking, but at the bottom of the heart and soul is a calmness and coolness.

Getting your mind trained and out of the way so you can experience this connection is magical and mysterious to a human being. It's a miracle when there are no thoughts dominating or controlling you. They begin to subside as there is a way for them to pass through you now, not being restricted to the point of imprisoning you with the obsessive thinking. It's a blissful moment when there is no more fear, but power, love, and stillness.

Immediately, I found peace at night, instead of having to numb myself with alcohol to cope with the pain. It was a miracle to be able to feel the strength from my true source that was taking the pain away and dissolving it. I started sleeping on the blow-up air mattress in the family room for six-to-eight hours a night. There was nothing like sleeping like this for months from all the effects of the separation and divorce—but that is another book!

The days and weeks after that were miraculous. I started to see life with a new lens, far beyond my 20/20 vision prescription. Everything was so crisp and clear, full of life. Nature, people, animals, situations, and circumstances all started showing up and appearing differently. It wasn't perfect though; it was a process, just like everything else you start, and it took time to master and reach full maximum-strength benefits. It's like taking two aspirin or ibuprofen for pain: it takes a while for it to kick in.

I remember all the raging emotions associated with me realizing I was at the end of a twenty-year marriage; the arguments, chaos, confusion, and hurt are still raw, like a fresh new wound that is bleeding profusely.

I continued to deal with the underlying pain and suffering from the abuse, and even though the light of the sun was shining in my life once again, darkness still took over at certain moments. I was learning how to remain in the light, even when I was in the darkness. However, meditation practice continued to be a gravitational pull back from those trying moments to get me back to the center of calmness and coolness.

One thing I began to connect with greatly was the beauty of myself and other human beings and the miracle of creation. I find it to be an amazing miracle when you can see another person as beautiful no matter what they look like or what they do. They're a human being, just like you, longing to be loved and accepted just as they are. Hugs, smiles, and kisses all come from a place and space of total presence. They have the power to heal and shine light like the marble into one's soul, no matter what soul and heart-level trauma and devastation persists.

It took me a while to realize I was a beautiful creation the moment I was created in my mom's womb. I was born on March 23rd, 1976, in the bi-centennial year in which America gained its independence on July 4th, 1776. I have a strong connection to freedom and independence, which every one of us as human being longs for, but it becomes lost over the course of life's journey through the struggles, challenges, and traumas. It's easy to become lost in a void and not know how to connect back to the miracle of true authentic self that is our birthright ordained from God. He has made each of us unique and special.

Seeing me now, at forty-four, I connect with my core DNA of fire, passion, and determination. I can tell you, that night when the sperm hit the egg must have been a wild, fiery, passionate night for my mom and dad for it to have called me forth into the world!

I was over a ten-pound baby when I popped out of the womb. I'm quite certain my mom can share a lot about the pain and suffering moments of my birth, but that's her own traumatic experience! I don't remember being born in that moment, and you wouldn't either. However, it is powerful to watch a baby open its eyes for the first time and start connecting with its surroundings and other human beings as they explore and discover.

Those are precious, miraculous moments for a man or woman to be a part of. I can attest to that, as God granted me the opportunity to help create and witness the birth of my two, amazing sons. What I found is that childbirth and being a part of it, along with witnessing it, is the ultimate, greatest miracle one can experience while living on this planet. This fact is that you're born into this world with a calling on your life with a unique purpose to fulfill. You are a beautiful masterpiece that is fearfully and wonderfully made. The Creator even knows the number of hairs on your head. However, I hope He has a tally sheet accounting for all the hairs I've lost over the years.

Quite simply, I realize that you and I are a miracle!

The moment of connecting to nature's finest, whether it be trees, grass, flowers, birds, or any other type of animal is amazing. I recall sensing the lushness of the green grass in the late spring, and in the early summer season seeing the green tree leaves and feeling a different connection with them. It was like I hadn't noticed them before, but I could really feel the energy of the plants, trees, and flowers radiating in their own respective beauty again. I'll never forget being able to connect to one of my favorite flowers, a rose bush, and to be able to see down into the pistil and veins in the leaves of the bud for the first time. The visceral power of the red rose petal color being infused in it and spreading out like dye. Whoa, what a powerful moment of connection to the full, pure energy between me and the blooming flower! It felt like I was a baby opening my eyes for the first time and seeing something completely new.

I'll never forget the moment of connecting with two Golden Doodles, Sammee and Ginger. I saw them as beautiful, adorable, lovable energies, rather than another thing to take care of, take to the vet and groomers, pick up, or clean up after, or see them as a pain in the rear end with their muddy feet all over the floor. Not to mention, Sammee being sprayed by a skunk three times in three years! It's amazing to connect with that playful energy in a whole new way and to appreciate and see their true spirit. Quite frankly, it was refreshing to realize they are truly man's best friend.

Most importantly, I discovered that in every moment of life is an opportunity to be and experience the miracle that you are. A birth of a child, the rebirth and restoration of a soul, and every moment of expressing and living from a surrendered and vulnerable self provides a supernatural connection to the higher self and power. Once I truly understood the miraculous creation that I am and my genuine, pure, authentic self, I discovered the true supernatural power and strength deep within me. In this discovery, I saw that I could create, imagine, and dream again into fulfilling my destiny's calling. There were no limits for what was possible for my life, just like there is a power for you to dream and create the life that you want.

As humans, in our limited thinking and beliefs, we often think miracles no longer happen, or at least, there is no way possible for us to ever experience one. We hear in biblical teachings that miracles happened long ago. Today, we hear of lives being saved by someone's heroic efforts, or modern medicine and technology, or some divine intervention to heal or protect one from harm. In the past, I always related to miracles in that way—until now. I've come to realize that I *am* a miracle that is here to serve and connect humanity with love, peace, and joy through the beauty of surrendering to life and vulnerability. The miracle of moving forward with a passion for courage, to create the life I want, and pursue my dream of helping humanity heal itself through its own awakening.

Over the last two years of my journey, I've finally had a transformational breakthrough from living life locked up in the handcuffs of my trauma. Now, I'm ready to help you become the person you were meant to be and cast aside all the emotions that rage within you from years of misunderstanding.

YOUR
EFFECT MOMENT

Think about that still, small voice—that calm, cool foundation within you that has always been there—that has been blocked by all the trauma, the darkness, the challenges, the struggles day to day, year after year.

• I wonder, what is there for you to discover in that still, calm presence within yourself?

Let's do a little connection exercise. I want you to look around for the nearest light—sunshine if you're outside, or the nearest light on the inside. As you connect with that light, breathe in for a count of four and visualize it filling you up. Then, on the exhale, I want you to breath out to a count of six and see yourself breathing out the darkness, the stress, whatever negative emotion is present. Do this exercise for a few minutes, all while staying connected to the light. Put aside the trauma, the hurts, the pains for just a moment to connect yourself to the beautiful, fearfully and wonderfully made human being that you are. I want you to say aloud, "I am a miracle." Say this over and over for at least a minute.

• Check in with yourself as you stay connected to the light. What is it that you notice about yourself after this moment of saying and recognizing that you are a miracle?

Chapter 7
The Grassroots: the moment of running home

For the following six weeks since starting my meditation practice, I learned so much about myself in that silence and stillness. The journaling and reflecting, sitting on the park benches, walking in nature at parks, all served as moments to reconnect with myself. In those moments, I discovered what I wanted for my life to start moving forward. I still had tears, although they felt like they were making me stronger every time one was shed. So, tears of strength, not sorrow anymore!

I remember one powerful moment. I had pretended and put on my smiley, clown-like facade face for so long. I had to make a declaration of something powerful that could become a guiding principle for my life to move forward. I wrote in my journal, "If it is not real or authentic, if it no longer serves what I want for my life going forward, then I don't want it!" This was mainly focused on all my relationships with people, but I started applying this in all critical areas of my life where I was investing my time, energy, and efforts on a day-to-day basis.

Being my nature as a man, I was always wanting to fix things, and I was trying to save the family from separation and divorce. I knew it was going to be severely hard on my kids, so while trying to restore the marriage was an option, it was also a major undertaking. At one point, home became so intense, I reached a point of no return, and I had to leave.

It was for my own best interest and wellbeing at that point. I no longer felt safe after my air mattress wound up with a nine-inch slit in it. I was told the dog must've mysteriously popped the mattress, but I believed otherwise. So, I spent the next day, Monday, contemplating what to do. Finally, by afternoon, I made the decision to leave once I got home that evening. I called the lawyer the next day and chose to file the divorce paperwork.

I had lots of thoughts—like, "Where am I going to go?" So, I called my mom and dad that afternoon after work as I was heading to get my stuff and said, "I'm coming home to live with you all." I knew, no matter what, I had a place to call home and be welcome with open arms. A moment I thought, at forty-two- years old, I'd never be faced with. However, darkness and brokenness have a way of bringing you back home, not just where you grow up, but also into the depths of your heart and soul. One thing I knew at this point was that God *never* leaves you or forsakes you! It is in the broken and contrite heart that God meets you right where you are to sustain and restore you back to your true authentic self—our grassroots glorious inheritance.

So, I packed up my car with all of my clothes and my stuff needed to live, and then came the hardest thing I've ever had to do in my life—telling my boys I was leaving. It was a gut-wrenching moment that I'll never forget, looking my two kids in their precious, hurt eyes, with their anger raging, and telling them I can no longer be there, that I don't feel safe and must go. I told them, "I love you both, and I'll be getting you to spend time together as your mom and I work through the next steps in the coming days and weeks."

The thirty-five-minute drive to my parent's house back in Pleasureville, Kentucky seemed like an eternity, as I was shedding many tears, feeling absolutely exhausted both emotionally and physically. It felt as though I was a towel that had been put through a wringer. As I approached the rocky, curved, and winding driveway, I instantly felt a connection back to those grass roots. I hadn't felt this connection in the many trips to their house over the years. As the tires crushed the rocks, I noticed they didn't actually end up crushed, but the rocks were standing strong on their foundation. I was back home to stand firm in building a new foundation. The focus was to start moving forward in my life.

It was an amazing moment of connection, of getting back to the grass-roots of being home, on our family farm, with cattle grazing in the field, rolling hills, and beautiful, lush, green, wooded trees and thickets surrounding their house. As I pulled in the driveway, my mom and dad were there to greet me with their beautiful, chocolate labradoodle, Kizzie. As I got out, tears of sorrow, joy, and uncertainty seemed to fade away as my mom and dad met me outside the car to wrap me with hugs and love. I'll never forget what they said, "Welcome home, Son, it's been a long time coming! You're home now and have a place here as long as you need it." I burst out in tears, knowing that, for the first time in years, I was safe, which was something that had been destroyed when I realized the devastation of the abuse.

I also remember my mom saying, "I have your room all set up and ready for you. What do you want to do with all of your clothes and stuff?" I said something profound that I'd started connecting back to my true self. I told her not to take them to my room and to stack all my things in the dining room for now, saying, "It's time to purge. Not just the clothes, but everything that no longer serves me going forward, including relationships with people who drag me down into negativity."

A cleansing and purification process of the heart and soul. A losing of the attachment to things and people. This included all material posses-sions, relationships, and things I had attached myself to that served no purpose at the end of the day. When I went through all my clothes and filled two, big, leaf bags full of clothes that my ex-wife had gotten me was one of the best feelings that drove a hunger in me for even more purging, cleansing, and purification. Wow, what a powerful moment of release and freedom that brought forth! That created a heart and soul longing for so much more stuff to purge out of my life, including the things I'd been attached to that were not healthy and only served my lust for more, more, and more.

So, over the coming days, as I got rid of more things and continued practicing meditation, reflection, and journaling of what I wanted for my life, I connected with this practice of minimalism. I started getting rid of so much stuff and kept only the bare minimum, the essential things to live. That included drawers filled with clutter and useless things that meant nothing and just sat there, taking up space to the point where I couldn't even open and close the drawer without rummaging my hands through the crap first, just to be able to open it. I was drawn to this other guiding principle: you don't need a lot to live and be happy and content when you find that contentment from inside yourself first. This is the shift that started happening by me connecting to my true, authentic self, which craved simplicity and choosing careers, material items, people, and relationships that aligned with this.

It brought me back to the connection I have with freedom and independence. It was like I took lemons, and instead of making lemonade, I started scrubbing the inside of my heart and soul in a beautiful, sanctified cleansing.

I remember I began to feel childlike and playful again as I spent more and more time back home. I'll never forget the moment I celebrated my sister, Stephanie's, birthday on September 25th. It was a Saturday afternoon, and I decided to just ride with my parents. We had a fun time connecting and celebrating Stephanie's birthday, and then, it was time to leave. I got into the back seat of my dad's beautiful, Kentucky-blue Ford-150 to go home. My brother-in-law was standing on the front porch as we were leaving, and I rolled the window down. I said, "Dude, there's nothing like being forty-two-years old on a Saturday night and going home with your parents." Then I turned to my dad and tapped him on the shoulder and added, "Dad, will you take me to go get some ice cream?" We got a good, big laugh out of that! I found laughter to be a great medicine for the soul.

In all the playfulness and fun, feeling somewhat childlike again, there was still the obvious turmoil of ending my marriage. I had moments of intense emotions that came with letting go of a relationship after a twenty-year investment with one person. As I continued the journey over the next couple of weeks, I came to the realization it was time to confront and heal from the sexual abuse.

I started running in the late summer and fall season while I was back home. Taking back your health and wellbeing is just as important as your mental healing. I'd discovered two important things by connecting back to myself and my grassroots: if I don't have my health or peace of mind, then what do I truly have to give to anything or anybody in my life? So, you should make yourself a priority and focus on these two things, as well. I was meditating twice a day, which grew me in peace of mind, and then, it was time to take my health to a new level.

I'd been in such a turmoil over the last several weeks and months that I'd lost connection with running, which is one of my favorite things to do for health, besides eating healthy and weight training. So, I decided to start back running the road that led to my church. That road had once brought me such intense pain and sorrow every time I passed the place where the abuse had happened. The road is Union Baptist Church Road. I absolutely hated that road.

The first time I went running there, I felt a bit of apprehension, nervousness, fear, and anger rising, as I ran past where that barn with the basketball goal and the two trailers sat parallel to one another. From the time of realizing the abuse, I'd always loathed traveling that road to church each Sunday. Plus, I wondered why I was even in church, trying to make sense of why God had allowed the abuse to happen.

My feet were hitting the pavement, and I grew anxious over what was going to come up as I turned that corner in the road and saw where the abuse had happened. I really didn't know what to expect, so as I hit that spot on the run, I remember stopping, with sweat pouring off my body, as the flashbacks started. I could see it all so clearly—the barn, the trailer, the man, the teenager, the moments of the darkness, the lies, the manipulation, the playing on my purity and innocence for six months.

I froze in the road. The barn was now gone, along with the two trailers. The man who'd abused me had died years ago. Despite those things, I had chills and sensed a coldness deep in my bones. I felt paralyzed. I said to myself, "I don't know if I can do this." Do what? Run by this place where it had all happened? It had been buried so long and suppressed deep within me that I didn't know if I could open those wounds again. I looked around, wondering and confused, with a racing heart. I asked myself, "What am I going to do with this here, now?"

After looking around for a bit, I took a deep breath, knowing I must die to this, so I could live. After a little over thirty years, I was finally at that fork in the road. I had to confront it head-on to move forward. After a few more deep breaths, I connected to that practice of meditation. I began to feel all the negative emotions and racing heart subside just a bit. As I continued to breathe, I imagined myself breathing out the darkness and inhaling the light.

I looked heavenward on that late summer, early fall-like day: a bit humid, sun rays beaming, crystal-blue sky. I reconnected to that moment of my epiphany under the bridge. Then, I stood in the road, and I just started declaring my power, freedom, and transcendence over and over, until something happened. I heard and felt deep within me, that voice saying, "It's time for you to run again, run that race in your own power, freedom, and transcendence. Forget what lies behind you and reach for only what's ahead!"

As I looked back up in the sky, I noticed a buzzard flying low and circling, which we were convinced had been my grandfather, who had died in March of 2003. We had buzzards circle our property continuously, like guardian angels looking out after us, showing his true love for his family and beautiful farm. As I connected with this buzzard, I started running again down that road and to the church. The bird maintained its path in the sky and followed me as I ran.

When I arrived at the church, there was a prayer garden that had been dedicated to my grandfather, Deward Stivers, who'd served as deacon of the church and had been a true, humble servant. I sat down on the bench and started crying uncontrollably as I felt his presence and God's whispering in my ear that it was going to be all right. I immediately connected with one of my favorite scriptures, Jeremiah 29:11—"For I know the plans I have for you, plans not to harm you, but plans to prosper you and give you a hope and a future."

But there was something different in these tears and the weeping. They didn't feel like tears of sorrow anymore, but those of strength; a supernatural strength to move me forward in my life to my true destiny calling—a call home to be and live in my true authenticity and presence to create and inspire and serve humanity in a way it has never been served before. It was the ultimate calling to continue healing my heart and soul, so others can heal theirs from the destruction and devastation from abuse as well. This started my next level of healing, not just from the separation and divorce, but from the sexual abuse that had broken me all those years ago.

The hard part of connecting back to grassroots and not forgetting where you come from, for me, was the hard work and what ultimately created the work ethic I have today. My dad had always advocated that there is no time to lay in bed and sleep. On the farm, you get up early and go to work, and that was often the case for me. I even remember the same holding true after a Friday night of playing football in high school, then waking up early on Saturday morning sore, beat, and banged up to hit the fields to work. I recall praying and thanking God many times for the rain, so I could sleep in and not have to work after the Friday games.

What this did for me was build a spirit of resiliency to bounce back from life's hard times. I once had a coach in high school who told me he believed "I'd run through a brick wall" when it came to playing sports. I am tough, I am determined, and I will not back down from any challenge or calling that I must rise to! So, I knew I had been built for the days, weeks, and months it would take me to reach the next level of healing. I knew it would take a lot of hard work, dedication, and getting up and moving every day to accomplish anything worth having. Reclaiming your power and creating the life you want and deserve is worth it!

As you connect to your grassroots, not just geographically but physically, emotionally, and spiritually, you might be sensing a longing for that true, authentic self in that connection. In your moment where you declare something powerful for yourself like "If it is not real or authentic, I no longer want it," think:

- What do you truly want for yourself?
- How do you see yourself having whatever it is you want?

Part 3
Continuous Healing of a Heart and Soul

As I continued processing the abuse, the hurt, the pain, and the big gushing hole in my heart, a big shift in my energy came. It was a lot like what shifts for a toy marble or architecture and art marble as it continues to move along in the process of being formed through a lot of heat and pressure. This is somewhat like shifting the energy state in a human being to begin transforming oneself to be authentic, natural self.

For my little eleven-year-old heart and soul to heal, it required a shift of energy to continue to come into that strong awareness, commitment, and action to move forward. This process involved a true connection back to me and a total self-expression that felt safe and pure. A transformational shift was happening in the energy state of my body by way of connecting to the whole self—mind, body, and spirit. This deep, spiritual connection back to my true self was like a marble's metamorphosis.

Chapter 8
Patching a Hole in the Heart

Coach: Welcome back! It's so great to see you. I'm excited for our time together today as I see all the work you've been doing over the last couple of weeks with connecting to yourself by breathing and saying positive things about yourself. As we step into today, there's something that is here for me.

Derrickeboy: What's that?

Coach: Did you ever watch Winnie the Pooh when you were younger?

Derrickeboy: Yes, I like Winnie the Pooh.

Coach: There's a saying that hit me this week about who you are. I can't recall it exactly. It says something like this: Always remember this about yourself and never forget it, that you're braver than you think, stronger than you feel, and smarter than you know. How does that land for you?

Derrickeboy: I am brave. I am strong. I am smart.

Coach: Yes, you are, and again, it's an honor to serve as your coach! *They fist Bump.* Now, Let's jump in and get started today. What's opening up for you from our last session and your experimenting with breathing and saying positive things about yourself?

Derrickeboy: It feels like the hole in my heart is healing.

Coach: Wow, that's amazing. Check in with yourself for just a moment with a couple of deep breaths. What does it feel like?

Derrickeboy: A patch is being applied.

Coach: Where is the patch being applied?

Derrickeboy: On my heart.

Coach: I just got this visual of the patch. It's like a bluish grey patch, like the color of your eyes. There are these drops being applied to the patch. It's like... Have you ever seen that heavy duty glue that sticks anything and everything together?

Derrickeboy: Yes, I have. I've used it to glue back my toys at times.

Coach: So, I see this glue—let's call this glue your spiritual glue—and these drops are being applied to the bluish gray patch. What do you see?

Derrickeboy: The patch is a circle and the drops are pure white.

Coach: Circular with pure white drops... I'm curious. What do the pure white drops on the circular patch represent?

Derrickeboy: The glue... *He laughs.*

Coach: Yes, certainly... You're funny! Let me point you back to this for you to explore what those drops could be. Just a moment ago, I mentioned what I recalled from Winnie the Pooh, and you shared what it meant for you. What did you say?

Derrickeboy: That I am brave, strong, and smart.

Coach: Indeed... Now, with those things you just said about yourself, what are the white drops on the patch?

Derrickeboy: Oh, you mean, are the drops being brave, strong, and smart?

Coach: Absolutely! What else?

Derrickeboy: I'm not sure... *He ponders for a moment.*

Coach: Did you bring your foam ball where you've been writing positive words about yourself on it from our last couple of weeks of work together?

Derrickeboy: Yes, here it is . . .

Coach: Okay, what are all the words on the ball?

Derrickeboy: Courage. Power. Free. Whole. Fun. Playful. Joy. Peace. Rise. Healing. Pure.

Coach: So, now, what do the white drops on the blue-gray circular patch represent?

Derrickeboy: All of those things.

Coach: That's beautiful! You're so creative! However, I noticed that you missed one, an extremely *important* one. Before you discover it, I want you to visualize this: you have your spiritual glue, and this one is not a pure white drop on the patch, but a continuous, circular, pure-white line that connects all the other white dots you just made. Go ahead and connect all the dots with this glue now... What is the line that connects all the other drops together?

Derrickeboy: I don't know.

Coach: Here's a little hint I picked up on when you read the words off the foam ball. You missed the back side of it. Rotate it around, and what is the word?

Derrickeboy: Oh, the most important one. *LOVE*!

Coach: That just gave me cold chills! Now, as you hold this patch in your hand, what are you noticing now?

Derrickeboy: A longing.

Coach: A longing for what?

Derrickeboy: To patch the hole in my heart.

Coach: That sounds like a new choice for you.

Derrickeboy: Yes! I so LOVE me now as my little Derrickeboy self, all of it—the wounds and scars! Let's give us a BIG HUG now!

The coach wraps his right hand over his heart and places the left hand over the right one.

Coach-Derrick: So, Let's play a little game on our favorite court!

Derrickeboy and Coach-Derrick: Okay!

Coach-Derrick: Let's go out to our basketball court to play our new game and bring our foam ball with us!

Derrickeboy & Coach-Derrick: Okay!

Coach-Derrick: So, here we are on our basketball court with the ball. I'm going to go over here and lower the rim down for us! Remember, we cannot jump! *They laugh.*

Derrickeboy and Coach-Derrick: What are we doing?

Coach-Derrick: Okay, let's go over here to the half court now! As we stand at the half-court line, I want us to imagine for just a moment that we're standing in Rupp Arena, where our favorite basketball team plays. I want us to pretend like we're dribbling the ball, and this represents the new commitments and actions we want to make to move ourselves forward. However, I don't want to cross the line yet into our home-side of the court. Stay over here on the opposing team's side for a bit. Got it?

Derrickeboy and Coach-Derrick: Yes!

Coach-Derrick: Why do we want to say "yes" to go forward?

Derrickeboy & Coach-Derrick: We say "yes" to patch the whole in my heart with my circular, white-drop line connected spiritual glue.

Coach-Derrick: Great! What else?

Derrick-boy and Coach-Derrick: We say "yes" to work hard to continue healing myself and discovering new things.

Coach-Derrick: Like what?

Derrickboy and Coach-Derrick: Remember that discovery exercise we did to start coaching, where nothing really opened for me with discovering my purpose, values, and inner leader.

Coach-Derrick: I remember like it was yesterday.

Derrickboy and Coach-Derrick: We say "yes" to not just discovering our purpose, values, and inner leader, but to also living them out every single day to fulfill our purpose of helping and serving other people.

Coach-Derrick: We are *amazing*! Now, what are we going to say "no" to here?

Derrickboy and Coach-Derrick: We say "no" to the power the abuse and darkness had over our heart. We say "no" to giving our power, strength, and courage over to anything and anyone else, only the supernatural and greatness that lives in us.

Coach-Derrick: Okay, when we're ready, I want us to cross the line! Here Derrickboy, jump on my back! Once we cross the line, we will declare our "yes" commitments, and then, run as fast as we can with our ball and dunk it so hard, it shatters the backboard! Ready?

Derrickboy and Coach-Derrick: Yes. On the count of three... Three, two, one...

We cross our half-court line and run as fast as we can and dunk it, crushing the background, and all the crowd of humanity bellows out deafening CHEERS!

Coach-Derrick: I LOVE US so much! I have one final challenge here. Will we explore and discover our ultimate purpose with our values and inner leader to rise above, take a stand, and transform ourselves through serving all of humanity who are experiencing hurt and trauma from any abuse—especially sexual abuse? We can accept, deny, or counteroffer.

Derrickeboy and Coach-Derrick: WE ACCEPT!

Coach-Derrick: We are so full of love, courage, peace, and joy now, and I know that God has a special purpose and unique calling on our life.

I, a forty-four-year-old man, coached my eleven-year-old Derrickeboy-self from a space of darkness and torture to a new space of nurturing to move forward in life. This involved bringing a balance of new choices, commitments, and actions to evoke that transformational energy shift to take place.

My coach trainings and techniques were learned through utilizing the Co-Active[1] coaching model. Now, I no longer allow my eleven-year old, wounded self to own and dominate my life going forward. I had to nurture him with love and compassion, while giving him enough space so true passion could shine bright out into the world to influence and serve humanity. This all centered around my ability to invest time, energy, and focus to evolve myself into my authentic, true, unconditionally loved self. True love is the essence that covers all things as we heal from the not-so pleasant and gut-wrenching life experiences.

[1] Co-Active Model Appendix Reference

As you connect to that gaping hole in your heart and soul, and you think about your spiritual glue-like moment,

- Describe the patching process for repairing the hole in your heart.
- What do you see as patching that hole in your heart today?

Chapter 9
The Sun: the moment to rise above

As I connect back to that moment in the garden at Union Baptist Church as God and my grandfather's presence spoke directly into my broken heart, I noticed what felt like a fresh, new scent rising from within me. It was an aroma like the smoke billowing out of a wood-burning fireplace. The dwarf magnolia trees were in full bloom igniting a sweet scent. It invoked a precious fiery passion deep inside my heart and soul to evolve and rise higher to the next-best version of myself. The *me* I wanted to give out to the world.

I know to rise higher demanded much of me—a lot like the hard work the farm and sports had required. The greatest discipline was to never give up, no matter what I was faced with in life. It took all the resiliency, grit, and determination I had.

The days ahead were filled with a whole new world of exploration and discovery. I had some amazing breakthroughs, but I also had many dark and painful moments as I continued undoing myself from the abuse and the loss of my marriage.

I awakened most mornings and sat on my parents' front porch to a beautiful sunrise, shining and rising its brilliance across the rolling hills of our farmland. I felt such a connection to those moments. The dew rising from the ground as it was being pulled up and lifted by the rising sun. The horses and cattle grazing in the pasturelands connected my heart and soul to a rising energy within to start the day. I watched the settled Amish community in Pleasureville, Kentucky ride their horses and buggies up and down the road, especially on Sunday mornings, and their beautiful horses exerted their energy in pulling their buggies. I connected back to the simple, authentic living of not wasting my energy on the busyness of all the demands of life. Like the horse pulling the buggy, I realized the importance of prioritizing and utilizing my source of energy wisely.

The walks in nature on our fifty-five-acre family farm were amazing. I specifically recall a couple of instances where I learned the power of a healing silence and letting the light beams through the trees fill me up. There is a creek on the back of our family farm that sits directly between two, rising, steep hills with beautiful trees—specifically, cedar trees. That arising aroma of cedar offered a soothing, warming touch on the heart and soul. Like a deer panting for the water, oh my soul longs for Thee!

I sat on a cut, tree stump in full upright position and started my meditation practice in the silent whispers of what nature had to offer, connecting to the flow of air in and out of my lungs. I could feel the sunlight beams peeking through the trees as it moved into its position. I felt that position deep inside me shift to that still, calm space—that voice deep within, now at home, resting. It felt so nourishing and blissful as I connected to everything that God had created around me and *for* me in that moment. A stillness spoke and connected me back to my pure heart and soul without my mind's activity constantly wanting to take me on its own roller coaster ride.

There was something about the light always being present, even when lying in the dark. I woke up the morning after connecting to the practice of daily gratitude and appreciation. It was 5:00 a.m. when I first opened my eyes and connected to the awakened state. As I started my daily gratitude moment, the first thing I noticed was the light shining through the darkness of the morning. I saw the light from the porch lamp in the yard shining through the window, letting me know it was there.

I proceeded with listing the three things I was grateful for in that moment, like the fact that I was breathing and alive— which some days was all I had! I was grateful for my father's generous heart. He'd just brought me a cup of coffee, showing how much he cared. I was grateful for my parents providing a place I could call home again, with lots of love, support, and hugs. I was grateful for my persistent, beautiful mom's heart going above and beyond—even at times, a bit *bossy*. It's so therapeutic to have people around you who care, nurture, and love you in the good times and the bad.

On to what I appreciated as I focused this on a challenge I was faced with. I appreciated that I was being taught patience as I healed from the abuse and the end of my marriage. I was waiting patiently as God's perfect timing showed everything to me as I remained in a surrendered and vulnerable state. Oftentimes, I tried to take things on my own willpower and strength but was met with resistance from others and situations that didn't work out. I quickly realized I was not in control of anything, and control only leads to frustration and disappointment.

Practicing this gratitude and appreciation discipline provided me the opportunity to also journal, reflect, and take time to meditate and read a devotional for thirty minutes to start my days. What I found so beautiful about these practices was they provided a moment to celebrate, offer praise, and connect to the divine within myself. It offered me a foundation for connecting back to myself each day. It was a lot like hitting restart on my computer to reboot me for the day.

Over time, I began to realize a lot of things about myself and what the next chapter of my life would be. I began to connect to my calling to use what had happened over the course of my trials to help others—to take the hand of unpleasant, losing cards I had been dealt and turned it around to win by serving humanity's healing in some way. That is when I started connecting with a wanting, a longing to create a coaching practice to connect people back to their true self and healing from the devastation of abuse and divorce. Quite simply, I found myself as just a gracefully broken servant at the altar set on fire to be a vessel to connect others to their supernatural power and greatness within themselves.

As I headed into the following holiday season in 2018, there was a lot of turbulence, like flying in an airplane with changing atmospheric conditions. I was being met with a spiritual battlefield of the mind. It was like a roller coaster of emotions. What an adrenaline-rushing adventure ride in life! It felt like this ride was being held together by a prayer and a bumper sticker. Thank God for the body harness lock on the seat and the disciplines I had started practicing—including the loving support of family.

However, the next big discovery I had made this easier. I started focusing on gifting myself, not with material possessions, but with internal gifts. For example, over the entire Christmas season, for two weeks I would grab a Word Business Plan Template and start building a plan for a coaching and consulting practice, which would eventually become Transcend Coaching and Consulting—which was the greatest gift of the holiday season I could have given myself. Creativity started to flow as I started brainstorming ideas, putting them on paper, and spinning some things into action.

I gave myself a huge Valentine's gift in February 2019, which I did not just give to my internal self, but eventually to others—like my family, community, and world. I signed up for the entire Co-Active[1] Coaching Training and Certification program that would take place over twelve months. That investment has been another one of the greatest investments I ever made for myself— not to mention how this has served others with their healing now with what has come out of that moment.

I have received a ton of external gifts over the years that were always tied to some tangible material item, such as the latest gadgets, clothes, homes, and cars. One day, though, I realized I had not given myself an internal gift to invest in becoming the next best version of me, such as meditating, signing up for coaching training, and branding a business. Some would argue this is selfish. However, look at the book I am writing now. All of this was part of that investment to be my best self, and I'm already touching and inspiring others' hearts and souls—all due to choosing to take a leap of faith and heal myself as a top priority and investing in my own, personal stock market.

Then, one day in March, I woke up. It was the 23rd, and I was forty-three-years old, a middle-aged man with a whole new vision and mission for life. I felt like I was twenty-three again as I was savoring every bite of my favorite, all-time cake— my mom's homemade German Chocolate. There's something about when you cut a ball and chain off your ankle and then can discover new freedoms and independence. You feel so connected, alive, and creative in this new energy. I realized how amazing that moment was—it was like I had received a rare golden ticket to tour the Willie Wonka Chocolate Factory.

The time had come to launch myself out into the world with a side business and establish my brand called Transcend Coaching and Consulting. I'm ready to rise, stand, and transform your life. So, I worked with a branding firm to create my business and start the process of building a website: *transcendwithtranscend.com*.

There is something special about the word "transcend" for me. As I started the practice of meditation on Father's Day, I found it to be a blissful moment of no thought and pure consciousness. It felt like I was rising higher, mounting up on the wings of an eagle, renewing my strength, and being in the presence of God. It was as if I could reach up and touch God's face. All exhaustion dissolved through my coming to Him to get the rest I had needed. It was like dropping a boat's anchor into the bottom of the ocean to secure the boat no matter what. Then, I dropped myself into the depths of the ocean of calmness, coolness, total surrender, and vulnerable safety!

As you connect to what is possible for your healing moments and as you process what healing looks like for your life, I want to connect you to the power of practicing gratitude and appreciation now and each day going forward!

- What are three things you are grateful for?
- What is a challenge or difficulty you're facing today?
- What do you see as something you can appreciate during this challenge or difficulty?

Chapter 10
The Anchor: the moments to stand up

I've found it takes an enormous amount of courage to stand up and heal yourself first. It's hard to explore and discover the path forward in life, given all the hurts, traumas, struggles, and challenging moments we all encounter. It's not like being the Cowardly Lion on the trip to Oz with Dorothy. It's like the lion that wakes up in the wilderness, knowing it's going to have to run faster than the fastest gazelle if he wants to eat. I must run a fast race to heal, and the time is now to share my transformation, hope, and inspiration with the world.

I ask myself another powerful question here, "Who is going to run faster?" My courageous self that is chasing my dream, serving as a catalyst for humanity's healing, or my cowardly self that is settling for a less-than-mediocre victim, full of hurt, pain, and trauma. The second is comfortable and takes the least amount of effort, and is often chosen by others in their lives.

I chose to stand up to run that race, which started in another one of those special cities to me on this journey that I now consider a part of my grassroots: Chicago, Illinois. This is where the magic, secret sauce connected me with all the Co-Active[1] coaching training courses. This consisted of being trained and coached by amazing Co-Active[1] certified leaders and other incredible, aspiring coaches. This was followed by another six months of Co-Active[1] Certified Professional Coach training in virtual classrooms, where expert-level coaches supervised us as we learned to coach clients ourselves. It's a model that brings a nice, delicate balance to a human's life. "Co" is equal to being, and "active" is equal to doing. It takes a lot of hard work and dedicated focus to push yourself to be your best and strike a Co-Active[1] balance to get back to your true, authentic self.

At the end of the day, we often run the rat race and hamster wheel of life and fulfill our connection quite well, *doing*, instead of being. This leaves us feeling empty, exhausted, burned out, and negative with anxiety, depression, and fear. It was in the dash of Co-Active[1] where the magic happened for me to understand the essence of who we are: human beings! After all, I had never heard us being called "Human Doings."

I remember the first trip to Chicago. I'd never been to a big city like that. I was a country boy from a small town, where there was lots of "Pleasure" happening... You can use your imagination there. I was landing at Midway Airport and seeing the city from afar, as we got ready to jump on the Orange Line. It was my first time being on a public transit system, so I know what you must be thinking!

Remember, I came from the glorious days of "Drive Your Tractor" to school day. It was an amazing sight to see all those tractors parked in the school parking lot as kids celebrated that special day. I was a sheltered country boy who married way too young, so I hadn't gotten to experience a lot.

So, I was stepping into this whole new space and world with jubilation. I remember thinking, "What on earth is a boy from small-town, dairy farm U.S.A. heading to a big city to do?" I would have never dreamt this for myself, but God always sees things differently.

A childlike playfulness moved me to explore and have fun. I hadn't connected to this side of myself since before the abuse. I soaked up every single moment and stepped into and up to the plate to swing the bat and play a new game. It was a great feeling to move forward into what I sensed was an authentic calling and connection to discover and explore new things about me.

I imagined myself standing on the back of a boat, looking down at the water and seeing an enormous anchor on a huge pulley-and-wire system. I felt it was time to start to anchor this boat and lower myself into a deep territory I never thought possible. Notice I said, *thought* possible. Limited thinking has a way of sabotaging people. I jumped from the boat and grabbed the anchor while feeling my hands tightly gripping and securely attaching to this anchor, as I was lowered into the water to discover new things about myself. It was nice to see other boats in the water— including elite, powerful boats that had already anchored along with me. These boats were the aspiring-coaches and elite, certified coaches who took a stand for one another and gave the space for, love, courage, and compassion. It was the opportunity to just show up freely, with no judgement, no assessment, and no expectations. I could explore and discover new things I needed to know about myself. I realized quickly that creating my new life was going to cost me the old one.

As that anchor was lowered down into the water to the bottom of stability, safety, and security for the boat, so was I lowered into the water to find the same over the next five months. Additionally, at the bottom lay the hidden treasure chest of life purpose, values, and inner leader to pour new concrete in my life again. These are all essentials to living and creating a fulfilled and content life that I so longed for. Holding onto that anchor was a tedious, lengthy process that had its moments of getting stuck, and stopping by its own friction.

Humans often get stuck, trapped, and feel like giving up on their paths to the bottom to find those treasures there holding strong, peaceful, stable energy. The anchor often moves again to continue flowing freely down to the foundational water's bottom, just as the energy in the cells of one's body often becomes unblocked through coaching, so that life can flow again freely, without resistance and restriction. I remember all those moments of being lowered like that anchor to discover my purpose, values, and inner leader.

As we worked with our elite-level- certified coaches on exercises in the course called Fulfillment[1], I was practically the poster child for the course—basically rearchitecting and recreating myself as though I was an old, outdated software system now ready to move to the latest update. It was an incredible opportunity to reinvent myself and find a purpose—that I am like an epiphany that unleashes power, freedom, and transcendence. Though, discovering that purpose will eventually shift to a new one. This shows the power of continuous exploration and being called to new levels on the journey. It evolves and changes as you become more aware. That's why it's always so important to be connected to yourself to begin with.

As I stepped into several exercises for values and the inner leader, I began to realize how much work I had done through all my journaling and self-reflection over my days of great struggles, including moving back home with my parents. Discovering and nailing down your value system and inner leader is like the milk one feeds a baby to help them grow. It's like a mining process, where you strike and find gold, or quarrying for marble below earth's crust. The day one truly gets rich, not by winning the lottery ticket or buying the right stock, is when they allow their values and inner leader to evolve over time and gain new insights and life experiences.

My values are to BE Simple, BE Authentic, BE Connection, Be Integrity, Be Compassion, and Be Love. As you connect with the stories that I have shared, you can see how it holds true that I choose what's important by aligning my purpose, values, and inner leader. This all happened once I got my old, broken, dark self out of the way to find my new self—one now filled with new energy, light, and hope.

Now to my favorite, most glorious inner leader. We call this our Inner Leader and Allies as we connect with an attribute of who we are called to be in every moment. It acts as our guiding compass, inner-gut instinct, or wisdom. For me, it is a connection to that "still, small voice." It serves as a human being's self-acceptance and self-authority, or being able to connect to that unconditional love and acceptance of yourself no matter the scars, wounds, struggles, and challenges. Take a courageous stand for the great self-power and authority deep within you to declare what you want for your life in an unapologetic, unwavering way.

I remember growing up and working in the garden with my granny, and we would plant the garden together each spring. One of my favorite things about it was taking a little-head cultivator plow attached to a huge wheel with two large wooden handles. We had a homemade one crafted by my grandfather. I'd watch him take that plow and mark the rows for the seeds of the beans, corn, cantaloupe, watermelon, cucumbers, etc. Then, my grandmother and I would go behind him and drop each of the different seeds into the cultivated row.

Once complete, we'd pull some of the dirt lightly over and barely cover those seeds, creating a perfect ratio of fertilizer, soil moisture, and sunlight to germinate the seed to become its own beautiful plant. One day, it would serve its purpose and deliver the perfect fruits and vegetables. I see cultivating these three, essential ingredients in a human being's life as no different. Those seeds of life; purpose, values, and inner leader and allies are essential for creating and living out a fulfilled and content life and serve as a guide to make a profound difference in others.

A powerful and transformational breakthrough happened in an August 2019 session, where I truly connected to forgiveness. I had been standing—surrendered and vulnerable—in front of the room with all twelve, aspiring coaches watching, and an elite coach guiding me through the principles of Resonate Choices, New Commitments, and New Actions as part of the Balance principle in Co-Active[1] coaching.

The new resonate choice for me to choose forgiveness, with a focused commitment to move myself forward. I'd been lying to myself over and over for several years about forgiving the several injustices I had experienced. That day, I was standing in front of the room, tears flowing, heart racing, with a lot of eyes on me. I declared something so powerful, I'll never forget it. I chose to *forgive.* Not because the man or anyone else deserved it, but because *I* deserved it! I deserved to be set free and reclaim the power and greatness inside myself, without anyone or anything else being able to rob me or hold the strings to my internal power, greatness, peace, and joy. Quite frankly, it enabled me to have an authentic expression of pure love again.

I love the relevance of a snakebite's venom to forgiveness. We all get bitten in life by this poisonous snake of betrayal—sometimes, by a spouse or partner, or abuse, or life, or business decisions—and that results in a negative outcome. It's not the bite of the snake that kills us. I found that it's the venom of negative, toxic, poisonous energy that continues to pour through us every hour of every day of every year that kills ours heart and soul and the authentic expression of who we are.

Forgiveness didn't happen instantaneously for me, either—it took a lot of time. Time that I was broken, humbled, and ready to surrender my will to God's. It took a moment to be called into that space and presence to forgive. At the end of the day, I choose to forgive so that I can have my fullest, most deserving, beautiful life of love, joy, and peace. I see these three things as our birthrights from the moment the sperm hits the egg. This is what we deserve in our life. So, having unforgive-ness in our heart and soul takes away our birthright and binds us up in toxic energy on all the days we choose not to forgive. Forgiveness is one of the ultimate transformational shifts that occurs in the heart and soul of a human being during healing. Remember, we forgive someone not because they deserve it, but because *we* deserve it!

As you lean into these essential life ingredients of life purposes, value systems, and ways to internally lead yourself forward in your life with the discovery of these things, think about,

• What do you see as possible for the anchors of life purpose, values, and your leader within to guide your life forward from where you are today?

I know forgiveness is a touchy subject. We all want to hold onto being right and making others wrong for an injustice, especially for victims of sexual abuse. Remember, we do not forgive because the abuser deserves it, but because we deserve it! Unfortunately, that snake has bitten you hard. Now, all that venom is pouring through you as toxicity and negativity day in and day out, year after year, and it's slowly killing you.

• What is it going to cost you long-term, if you continue to rob yourself of your power and freedom that you truly deserve here by not forgiving?

• What do you see happening for yourself if you choose to forgive?

Chapter 11
The Run: the moments of major transformation energy shift

I discovered that my major, transformation only happened when I decided to see differently, shifted my perspective, and connected myself back to a higher, spiritual energy—something that was much greater than me and beyond human comprehension. In this continuous process, as I worked toward discovering my true, authentic self by navigating through the struggles, barriers, and limitations, that all of it originated in how one thinks. As I thought like this, I found it was exactly how I saw things through those 20/20 lenses, which drove how I behaved and acted. It spewed out an energy that I wasn't aware came out of me, but others around me could sense, like body language, tone of voice, or words I used. They all created a certain perception of me to others.

Perception is one key to human interaction.

For example, all those negative, continuous thoughts from the sexual abuse I encountered—how I thought I'd never recover from the devastation, how I was a victim, how I thought there was no hope, how I internally argued over why it happened, and how I couldn't trust anyone —all led to me adopting certain behaviors, like putting on one of my favorite wrestlers, the Macho Man Randy Savage.

I related to the image he portrayed as a wrestler. He was a macho man with an obnoxious ego, protective façade, and a raging, bitter, angry energy that, with his constant winning, judging, and high profile, led him to think he was always right, and that everyone else was wrong. This ultimately resulted in a trail and footprint of negativity that served no one or anything.

There is also a major connection here to what I call the "law of attraction," as well. I discovered that I attract people and things by how I show up in life. Imagine a circle with five arrows around it. At the top of the circle is an arrow protruding down to the right—we will call this arrow, Our Continuous Thoughts—either positive or negative about yourself or others. Then, the next arrow of the circle, called Our Continuous Feelings, is created from the thoughts. Continuing toward the bottom, the next arrow is called Our Conditioned Behaviors, which all come from the feelings. Then, the next arrow is called Our Created Actions, which are driven from behaviors. Finally, the last arrow is deemed, Our Attracted Results, dealing with all people and situations.

Human Energy and Attraction

Results

Thoughts

Actions

Feelings

Behaviors

This continuous loop is exactly what creates human energy and emotion that protrudes outward to all things. This is where the rubber meets the road in living out either the fruits of the spirit of love, joy, peace, patience, kindness, gentleness, and self-control or the fruits of darkness in hate, malice, bitterness, rage, anger, blame, and judgement. Basically, the law of attraction just means that what one gives out of themselves, they receive back. In other words, you reap what you sow!

This is not only with people, but with animals and nature, as well. Ever wonder why a dog runs away, or cowers down from you, or why a flower withers and dies? Look within yourself to see what energy persists in that moment. Nature and people respond to energy by either running to or from it. I know this from firsthand, life experience.

I worked tirelessly, day after day, on this circle diagram by making lists of my thoughts, feelings, behaviors, actions, and results to document my major, fundamental, transformational shift in energy. This represented the principle of Process in my Co-Active[1] coaching training that focused on processing by releasing and shifting emotions. Simply put, I created circles with all those dark energies from the abuse, the divorce, along with all the negative energies, and called them out with new circles of corresponding fruit of the spirit energies that I wanted.

Then, I made a list of my corresponding behaviors and actions associated with each energy that lead to my major, fundamental shift I'd been waiting for. Amazing when this shift happened for me. I started showing up much differently to everyone and everything around me. I discovered a powerful connection to myself as a human being and leader. I was able to lead myself to attract what I truly wanted, which included bringing other people into my life who aligned to that same energy. I find if you want true love, then you must *be* true love. Vice versa—if you are angry, then you attract angry people into your life.

Then, one day it happened. I experienced another supernatural intervention while heading out for a morning run. I want to take you to another surreal moment I had in September 2019. It was during a Friday morning run while I was attending the last principle of the Co-Active[1] Coaching training and certification program, Process, for the weekend. As I exited the building on East Illinois Street in Chicago, I could feel my knees aching, my back tightening, and my negative self-talk of how it would have been so much easier to have stayed in bed for an extra thirty minutes. Finally, I snapped out of it while reminding and affirming myself that I was choosing health and wellbeing right at that moment. Then, I started observing the environment, the beautiful city of Chicago and its impeccable building architectures, construction crews, people, and cars. Of course, people's heads were buried in their cell phones, clueless and disconnected of who or what was going on around them. I also saw others out torturing themselves for this thing called health and wellbeing—like me!

I looked up to see dark, thick, raging clouds in the sky just as I was about three-quarters of a mile into the run, heading toward Navy Pier on Lake Michigan. When I arrived about a quarter of a mile from the pier, I immediately saw the sun rising through the clouds. I stopped for a moment to catch a few photos, and in an instant, I realized this was another perfect metaphor for my life's journey. That although there are moments when there are ominous clouds and storms in our lives, the sun, with its glorious rays of light, still rises and shines bright each day, no matter what.

As I soaked up that moment, I notice a zinging, pulsing energy going through every cell in my body as blood pumped fiercely within, feeding my body the oxygen and energy to run. Also, I picked up on this high sense of clarity and intent purpose. Everything felt so alive and connected, like bursting beams of a flashlight, shining bright as it navigates the dense, heavy fog for a clear path. I carried on with my run, so in tune with this powerful, transformative moment that nature was bringing forth. As I approached the end of the pier, after continuing to watch the beautiful, spectacular sunrise through the dark, rolling clouds, I noticed the glistening beams of orange light on the water. I had an intense urge to just start running on the water to the sun and rise even higher with it—like the miracle of stepping out of the boat and walking on the water kind of moment!

Suddenly, I was aware of this amazing, beautiful anchor on a concrete platform, sitting about four or five feet above the pavement, with a half-circle of American flags on several poles blowing gracefully in the wind. I felt an intense, strong connection to this eight-ton anchor from the *U.S.S. Chicago* at the end of Navy Pier, a staple in American naval fleet history that had served in the WWII, Korea, and Vietnam wars before being dismantled in 1984.

What was amazing about this anchor is it had been restored by a noble and honorable group of former sailors, who had reconnected through social media in 2012. I immediately felt a deep connection to liberation and restoration, an alignment to a new destiny calling of something much bigger than anything I could have imagined or dreamed for my life's journey; a reaffirmation of the calling by what God had already revealed to use my gifts, talents, passions, and voice to speak and serve others.

From my life's experience and transformational spiritual awakening, I want to share some beliefs I came to know in a powerful way. My beliefs now aligned to the conditioning from light, and not from the darkness. These have anchored me in life's journey to move forward with a dedicated, focused intentional purpose:

• I believe everyone has a powerful story that offers inspiration to humanity. You are a miracle and deserve to have your voice heard!

- I believe in grass roots and not forgetting where you come from. You are a beautiful creation, with a rich heritage and legacy to fulfill.
- I believe one is only at their best when authentic to their core. You must be who you truly are, and not what others or the world calls you!
- I believe there is a supernatural power, greatness, creativity, and destiny for one's life and purpose. These often get blocked by all the limits, cultural conditioning, and negativity from others' opinions and judgments, which robs you of living a fulfilling life. You are extraordinary—with special, unique gifts, talents, and passions.
- I believe in true love only when true vulnerability is present. The essence of who you are is only love!
- I believe it takes courage to stand up and take action to create what you want for yourself in the midst of life's challenges—like negative, horrific situations and others who devalue and degrade your worth as a human being. You are worthy and more than enough.
- I believe that one cannot give what they do not have within themselves first—like true love, peace, joy, happiness, contentment, and fulfilment— that only comes from an authentic connection with the self. You only attract what you are!

The call is now for me to take things to the next level through the power of creating from a pure heart and soul. It's time to dream, imagine, visualize, and manifest the next level of healing for myself and humanity. I recognize the stakes are high for all of us, and there is an urgency in the calling to further heal myself and *you* from the devastating effects of sexual abuse or other abuses and traumas. Ultimately, so we can be a vessel that is used to serve and support others in their healing, it's time to get busy creating from this new presence and space I found.

YOUR EFFECT MOMENT

As you connect to the energy state within you and whether the energy is positive (light) or negative (darkness), I want you to connect with the circumstances, situations, and people in your life today. When you reflect on these things and the possible impacts on your energy, I want you to write out your human energy and attraction diagram. This is your thoughts which may be driving the continuous cycle of feelings, behaviors, actions, and results for yourself.

- What are you noticing to be present in your life as you connect with your energy state within?
- What shifts for you if you start to think differently?
- What do you truly want to attract into your life?
- Then, who do you need to become?

Part 4
Creating from a Pure Heart and Soul

The colorful, shiny toy marbles emerge from the sack cloth or glass jar and are placed onto the smooth surface inside a circle. I wonder what they must be feeling now after being refined, quality tested, and approved for use. Finally, being made pure and whole to show up to fulfill their intended purpose. A purpose to unite kids and adults together in a competitive or playful way to engage in a game of marbles. A moment to connect to child-like imagination and purity.

As the architecture marble, either a precise cut or lengthy, rectangular sheet panel has arrived to be installed as flooring, countertop, or on a building frame, it knows its own creation to fulfill its purpose. A purpose connected to shine as a radiant light and durable enough to withstand pressure. That light of shiny radiance that draws and commands one's attention.

Both emerging with their own unique, special impact on the world. To be used to make a difference in their own respective ways. As I play with the toy marbles or admire the beautiful architecture of marble today, I sense a depth of connection to being refined. A refinement that feels empowering in an authentic connection to self.

After going through years of transformation, I can now fulfill my longing to be used to make a difference in others who have experienced sexual abuse.

I gained a deep connection back to Derrickeboy's purity and innocence to be creative, fun, and energetic, while using my voice to ignite and inspire others passionately to share their voice and heal. I transformed just like my precious marbles, and now I'm prepared to step into a coaching session with my hired life coach to connect with a new life purpose to fulfill a major calling to touch many people's lives with my story.

Chapter 12
An Emerging New Purpose and Supernatural Calling

Coach: It's great to be with you, Derrick, in our time today. I sense from all the work we've done over the last seven months, that we've reached a point in your healing journey where it's time for the next level. What is your topic today for our time together?

Derrick: It's like there's a burning fire raging within, like something needs to come out. Something is emerging about my purpose and calling.

Coach: I hear you wanting to explore a new purpose. Is that the topic for today?

Derrick: Yes, it is. And I want to leave our time today with a brainstorm vision of what it is.

Coach: Okay, so we landed the topic, and what you're wanting from today. What do you sense is emerging as the calling here?

Derrick: It's something big, and I can't seem to put my finger on it quite yet.

Coach: Let's check in with that inner leader of Soaring and your ally, the Eagle. As you connect with yourself soaring as an eagle, what is the eagle rising to?

Derrick: It's not rising. It's sitting in the nest high up in the tree, just waiting and looking out on the horizon. Like it's waiting patiently for something.

Coach: Waiting patiently for what?

Derrick: Where to fly to next!

Coach: So, let's do a little imagination work. Let's visualize you as an eagle sitting high up in this tree in your own nest. As you gaze at the horizon with that magnificent eagle's vision that can see for miles away, I want you to describe what it is you're seeing as you look out. Go ahead and close your eyes and visualize this moment... What do you see now?

Derrick: As I look out on the horizon, I see plenty of spacious, blue sky, lots of sunlight, lots of nature—like lush, green trees of many different kinds and powerful, raging waterfalls and calm streams. Then, there is this huge mountain that stands out.

Coach: That's an amazing connection to this visual. You are Connection right now. What is it about the mountain that stands out?

Derrick: It's like a huge rock ledge protruding out from about halfway up; it looks like a landing platform.

Coach: What else do you see?

Derrick: There's a burning fire all around this ledge on the mountain and that powerful waterfall to the left of it.

Coach: Wow, let's keep going! What's below this ledge and the burning fire and powerful waterfall?

Derrick: I see a lot of people gathered, searching for something through their silence, their hurts, pains, and sufferings.

Coach: I feel you have a burning desire deep within you to tell them something. What is it for you?

Derrick: There's something burning hot deep within, like a burning fire rushing down into the depths of my soul, or like a powerful waterfall needing to say something.

Coach: What is it you want to say?

Derrick: I see myself leaving the nest to fly over to say, "It's time for you to 'Wake Up' and heal yourselves."

Coach: Wake up and heal from what?

Derrick: The abuse, darkness, and devastation in their hearts and souls.

Coach: What do you see as your role here?

Derrick: To take a stand, be courageous, and share my story of how I am healing from the sexual abuse I experienced as a boy.

Coach: You are courageous and bold. I sense an urgency here on your part. What is the urgency I'm sensing?

Derrick: I long for those of abuse to restore their lives back to their true, authentic selves, with new purposes, values, and abilities to lead them forward in an ignited zeal and passion for life.

Coach: Who do you see yourself being as you use your voice?

Derrick: Surrendered, vulnerable, compassion, unconditional love.

Coach: What is important to you about this?

Derrick: My strong value of Connection.

Coach: There's something big-time emerging here in the supernatural universe. Like a new calling. I want to make a request here now. Will you find a colorful stone or rock that represents the burning fire and powerful waterfall you just described burning down into the depths of your soul, and take time to journal, reflect, and create a new purpose statement over the next couple of weeks?

Derrick: Yes, I'll do that and text you what opens as a result.

Coach: I have one more thing. This is a challenge from me to you. It's time for you to share your story to the world about the abuse and how you're healing from it! Will you write and publish a book within the next twelve months?

Silence for a minute.

Derrick: I've never written a book, and I'm a little hesitant to accept that challenge.

Coach: What's the hesitancy about?

Derrick: It's my own limited belief that I can write a book as I've never—

Coach: Let me stop you right there. You also thought, when we started this journey together, you could never heal from the abuse, and here you are today, by all the work you've put into transforming yourself to this place in time. So, you can do this. I *know* it. The time is now for you to step up to the plate and be a voice that breaks the silence. So, what's the answer? Yes, no, or counteroffer?

Derrick: *Sits silently for a minute.* Yes, I'll do it! I accept the challenge to write a book in twelve months.

Coach: Great! You are amazingly courageous, and I know it's going to inspire and touch the hearts of many! What do you need from me to support you on this?

Derrick: Just be available to read things as I start writing to share some feedback based on all the work we've done.

As we stepped away from the session, we both had a knowing deep within of what had just transpired because of the powerful tools in Co-Active[1] coaching model. By utilizing all the principles of Fulfillment[1], which involved imagination and visualization to lead to a new connection of a possible new purpose, values, and leader within. This shows the powerful evolution and expansion of a human transformation: a middle-aged man now fully connected and aware of how to continuously stretch, grow, expand beyond all limits of narrow thinking to a space of infinite possibility and a supernatural call to be used as a vessel to offer and shine brilliance for humanity's healing.

As you connected with a marble's journey and my life journey of transformation to be connected back to fulfilling a purpose, there's a moment for you to become aware of a possible transformation for yourself. Imagine a burning fire deep within and something needs to emerge out of you now to fulfill your purpose.

- What are you being called to do?
- What is your vision for living a fulfilling life?
- What does this give you going forward?
- How does this impact relationships, community, and the world around you?

Chapter 13
The Revolutionary Dream and Movement: the moments to upset the status quo to shine and serve humanity's healing

As I checked back the next morning and settled into my devotion and meditation time, I began to connect back to that creative, imaginative moment in coaching about the mountain ledge, the burning fire surrounding it, and the raging, powerful waterfall. I noticed a burning sensation like the fire and waterfall flowing freely and forcefully all throughout my body and down into the depths of my heart and soul. I was back to that zinging energy I had at Navy Pier in Chicago several months before in a moment of magical breakthrough and transformational shift in my life. I was experiencing that same energy, but more intense than ever. It was a knowing that something deep within was to be explored and discovered, so it could break free out into the world. It was like a new dream was not just emerging as something to long for; it was as though the dream was happening exactly as had been planned by the Universe.

I continued meditating, reflecting, and journaling over the next several days as what was inside was marinating like steak in my favorite marinade. I was patiently waiting for God to reveal exactly what was emerging within me—a new purpose, vision, or dream—as part of my longing to serve and make a difference in humanity. It was important to understand that I was learning on this healing journey that timing was everything. Also, it's important for me to remain in a surrendered and vulnerable state, not trying to force my own human agenda or understanding. It just wouldn't work out well when I would try in my own, human willpower. I was waiting patiently for the spirit to reveal to me exactly what this was.

I even tried to look around, even searching on Amazon for a stone or something colorful to connect with that might emerge and launch me into awareness of this new purpose and destiny calling. Then, after about four days, the moment occurred one evening after I had finished dinner and was just sitting on the middle of my bed. I was just chilling out, and I remembered I needed to get some paperwork out of a dresser drawer. I'll never forget that moment of opening that drawer— it was like a slow-motion video as time froze the moment my eyes landed on a mason jar full of marbles. I'd forgotten all about them, and it hit me— that moment when my grandmother handed me that jar. I can still hear what she said with her serious look and adamant tone of voice, "Make sure you promise me that you don't ever lose or give these marbles away. You're going to need them later in your life." I was jolted like a water hose had just sprayed my face on a cool, spring day. I stopped dead in my tracks and wondered what had just happened.

So, still feeling like I was watching a slow-motion video, I reached down and grabbed those marbles and pulled them out of the drawer. In that stillness, my grandmother's whispered words remained.

As I approached the bed, the white bedspread, so vibrant in all its purity, called me to sit down. I landed right in the center of that bedspread, and as I slowly touched the wire clip holding the lid snuggly on that jar, an overwhelming energy burst forth, so much so that tears swelled up in my eyes as I poured all the marbles out onto the bed.

I started admiring those round marbles— the many bold, subtle colors and different sizes— and I was drawn to this bluish one that grabbed my attention the most. As I connected with that, I remembered what my life coach had requested about finding a stone or some colorful object to connect with and put in my pocket as something special to me. I began playing with the marbles on the bed as those overwhelming feelings of pure, childlike innocence and playful energy washed over me. Of course, tears were flowing freely down my cheeks at this point; my tears were not sorrow or strength, but something different. Actually, as Ephesians 1:18 beautifully reminds me, "those were tears from the eyes of an enlightened heart and soul that now sees forth in hope to which He is calling me to, all of the riches of His glorious inheritance in His holy people." I discovered the new vision and dream, a destiny calling that night for me to shine bright like a marble.

So, I started journaling and reflecting on that powerful moment over the next couple of days. I felt like a kid on Christmas morning, longing and waiting to open those beautifully wrapped presents under the tree that Santa had just dropped off. As I began to unpackage them one by one, with every sentence I wrote, I finally opened the last present and found the gift from that imaginary-vision exercise I had with my coach.

A miraculous revelation struck me as an emerging purpose in that: "I am like a marble that shines brilliantly for humanity's healing." That burning fire on the mountain and the powerful pressure from a raging waterfall off that mountain represented all the heat and pressure. Exactly what had taken place in my life to lead to my metamorphosis to be like that marble and shine as bright as it does.

I discovered the power of imagination and visualization for a human being holds significant power in creating and manifesting what it is I want to create in my life. This took me one step closer to fulfilling my purpose and destiny calling as an inspirational speaker, author, and coach. Evoking this practice as a creative way to express my authentic self, as well as dream and connect me to a higher version of myself that was beyond human comprehension.

I passed the time as a child by standing on my grandparents' long, lengthy front porch, imagining and pretending to be a speaker on stage. I would snap a small limb off a nearby tree to serve as the microphone, drag a wooden stand from the toolshed for the podium, and turn the front porch light on to shine down on the porch. Then, the stage was set, and the moment had arrived for me to use my voice and speak, like Evangelist Billy Graham, whose crusades my grandparents had committedly watched over the years. A man who God used to speak and who touched millions of people over his lifetime.

As I spoke, I visualized having an arena full of people in front of me as I poured my little, child's heart and soul out with a fire, determination, and passion to land a message with my imaginary audience. As I came out of that imaginative state, back to reality, I would see my grandparents sitting in their colorful, green-and-yellow lawn chairs, smiling from ear to ear, cheering me on with words of affirmation and encouragement. I recall them both saying, at different times, "Son, you're going to speak and touch thousands upon thousands of people's lives one day."

Years later, as an author and speaker standing on platforms worldwide to share and inspire you, I know that dreams *do* come true. I connect back to those moments of using imagination and visualization of being a speaker—and now, an author—manifesting itself to fruition.

Another dream I had as a little boy was of me, on the paved, blacktop driveway, shooting hoops and hitting game-winning shots, as a star basketball player for the University of Kentucky, performing in front of thousands at Rupp Arena. Well, that was until I realized I couldn't jump! So, here I am, as an inspirational speaker and author, standing on platforms with all the bright lights shining on me.

With a racing heart and sweaty palms, I step into and embrace the moment to deliver a powerful and intriguing story of hope and transformation like no other. A message of power, freedom, and transcendence for when you choose to move beyond limited thinking and mediocre living, to seek and discover your true, authentic self and an abundant, unlimited, anything's-possible spirit. I now understand and appreciate grassroots, and the old saying, "One should never forget where they come from." All the unique and special traits I inherited were ordained by God as my being fearfully and wonderfully made—not to mention that dreams are my birthright, like seeking and finding "Waldo" on this life journey.

Being a new author and knowing nothing about authoring a book, I titled a page "Just Write from the Heart." I simply started vomiting my story out one page after another. The words just flowed out like a shower head being turned on every morning to start a fresh new day. Finally, I realized I needed some help after about a month. I got connected through a social media friend, who was an author, with a class that provided a structure for writing a book. From the insights and disciplines I learned over the course of eight weeks, I further refined and expanded on my powerful story through unleashing a hidden creativity deep within. This is exactly how *The Marble Effect* came to be. I never would have dreamed that as a new, first-time author, I would be launching a new book into the world in approximately eight months. What a humbling moment for a small-town country boy who only wants to truly share my voice, gifts, talents, and passions as a true servant-leader called by God to help other people heal from their abuse.

In October of 2019, I was finishing up the last coaching training, called Synergy[1], where I made a powerful, courageous declaration of living out and fulfilling my life purpose in the world. What I didn't realize at the time of owning my commitment to author the new story of my life was the start of a potential new movement—a stand for human beings suffering from sexual abuse.

I recall a special moment with another aspiring coach, right before we had to share our new commitment and declaration to the entire class on the last day of training. This gentleman intuitively turned to me and said that there was something deep within me that was about to be launched out into the world in a revolutionary way.

I said, "I can feel it!" Then he responded with three powerful words, "What is it?"

I pondered that question in silence for a bit before answering, but I'll never forget what I finally said: "I'm going to be a leader of a new movement—somewhat revolutionary—by taking a stand for every man, woman, boy, and girl—and race, any ethnicity—who has experienced sexual abuse."

We both immediately connected eye to eye and felt the bursting energy like rocket engines just fired up, preparing for launch. He commented that this was exactly what I was being called to take forth into the world.

As we ended that coaching session, I realized I had cast a whole new vision out to the supernatural Universe, and here we are, a year later, with *The Marble Effect – A heart and soul healing from sexual abuse.* I can't wait to see where it will be a year from now, in 2021.

There are a lot of examples of new, revolutionary movements, whether they're for a social community cause, religion, or politics. I'm going to keep it light and use one of my favorite fiction movie series of all time that created a movement from one voice that was able to touch and inspire many voices to join forces together for a cause worth fighting for. That is what a movement is all about. It's not about one person, but it's all about that one person being courageous enough to take a stand to unite and inspire the whole.

I love *The Hunger Games,* where Katniss Everdeen, or actress Jennifer Lawrence, starred in this series. Her courageous stand and authentic presence and voice from District 12, through her perseverance and sacrifice, brought forth a unifying presence of all the people across all the different districts. This was all for one purpose, to defeat President Snow and the Capital. You saw how her courageous stand, presence, and what she was truly fighting for ignited a revolutionary movement of all people from every district. She became known as the superhero, "The Mockingjay," with her own symbol that resonated and connected all the people together, uniting many voices behind the movement. The most amazing part of her as the superhero was that she came out of nowhere, merely volunteering to take her sister's place in order to accomplish a dangerous task. This showed her passion, authenticity, and courage to stand up and fight for the people she cared for. Her belief in herself made her a hero.

I've always looked at heroes as fictional characters like Superman, Spiderman, or a famous, extraordinary baseball, football, or basketball player. Of course, I have many sporting superheroes out there— with some of my favorites like Tom Brady, Michael Jordan, and Ken Griffey Junior, to name a few. However, in 2006, I fell in love with one of my all-time superheroes in what is called the "greatest two minutes in sports"—the Kentucky Derby. Derby 132 is an elite, talented group of three-year-old horses, one of the most talented groups to race in the derby.

That day, Barbaro stole the hearts of more than 150,000 fans in atten-
dance, not to mention those watching from across the world, that
which was deemed as one of the most amazing, superb performances
by an elite athlete ever. I want to take you to that moment where the
ultimate power, strength, and greatness within Barbaro took over. To
paint the picture, he was behind the field, around fourth to sixth place,
for the first three quarters of a mile in a mile-and-a-quarter-length race.
Then, on the outside final turn of the 132nd Kentucky Derby, he was
cruising steadily in a great outside position, guided beautifully by
jockey Edgar Prado as the field hit the final turn. He was in fifth place,
and in that turn, he hit another gear that none of the others had in
them. He went from fifth to take the lead, and won by approximately
seven lengths, which was something that had not been done in history
to make it an elite, superb performance. He captivated the hearts of the
fans and watchers—including *this* heart—across the world; all by how
he showed up and owned his own superpower, strength, and greatness
within to lead him to victory.

You may wonder why I say this. Behind everything that ends up cap-
turing the hearts of the people is a true, authentic presence to show up
courageously and win the race. This holds true in our lives today as we
connect with various movements in our society. In our case, to win the
race in our lives to heal from the trauma, the abuse, and the devastation. What I have discovered about a superhero that's so important is
that we are our own superhero. There is a great power and strength
that lives in us and through us each day—God!

So, as I connected with *The Marble Effect* as its own revolutionary movement, I wanted to share the vision of what I saw happening in the future
—all being ordained and created by a higher power. Remember, this all
started when my grandmother handed me a jar of marbles. This was like
a prophetic vision sent forth by a much higher power than any of us
could even begin to comprehend. Only God, in His supernatural way,

can create connections, special moments, and revolutionary movements in the right time and place. I'm only sharing what has been inspired and put into my heart to share and stand courageously as one voice connected to the superhero within me to deliver my story. A heart and soul healing can occur only when I choose to reclaim the power over my life and put the hard work and effort in to move forward.

Now that you've read this book, are you ready to lead yourself in the days, months, and years ahead, and to put the hard work into healing yourself from the devastating traumas and abuse in life and help me with this movement? In a sense, are you ready to discover the superhero inside you and go courageously to where you've never gone before? I believe in you, and I *know* you can do it!

I'll leave you with this final connection to *The Marble Effect*. As I shared the writing of this book early on with humanity, the outcry from others has been unbelievable. Unbelievable in that so many people, both men and woman, have shared that sexual abuse happened to them, and they'd never talked about it with anyone. They just buried it, let it lie dormant deep within in darkness, like that sedimentary rock.

People ask what I plan on creating for community support and assistance with healing, going forward. To answer that, I was inspired by another beyond-powerful moment that happened in San Antonio, Texas where I was at a conference sharing about writing this book. A middle-aged man, who'd never shared his own abuse while on stage speaking, shared his experience with sexual abuse as a child. Until that time, he'd never told *anyone*, including his family. All I could do in that moment was shed tears, tears that led me to give him a huge hug after his speech for his courage and voice. I asked him what had inspired him to share that, and he said that hearing my story had given him the courage.

This proved that it only takes one voice to ignite the courage of others to find their own voice and share their stories, as well. I've found that telling my story and writing it down in this book has provided me with an even deeper level of healing I never thought possible. So, this book has officially served its purpose for me, and I pray it has for you, too. I'm deeply grateful I had the courage to rise above the abuse and deliver a message of hope, inspiration, and transformation to others. It's truly been an honor and great healing to write the book and share and create from a pure heart and soul again!

So, I've connected you to a new revolutionary movement and what's possible for your life by telling you my story. A restoration of your purity, innocence, and a call for you to create what you truly want in your life. Imagine and visualize your healing and what that would be like to be free and connected to humanity to share your gifts, talents, and passions in service to the world.

- What do you want to manifest into your life now?
- What does this give you that you've so longed for all this time?
- How does this impact your relationships, community, and the world around you?

Chapter 14

From my Heart to Your Heart: a moment to inspire healing and declare completion.

Dear Beloved Human Being,

I want the final chapter and ending to be unique, unorthodox, and outside the box in its own special way. I'm writing my own love letter from deep within my heart to yours! Hear me when I say this, you may not feel loved and might not have felt love at all or for most of your life. That includes being seen and heard. I know the darkness, the pain, and the suffering you're enduring or have endured. I just want to say to you from my eyes of a sexually abused fellow human being to you, as my abused brother or sister's eyes, that I LOVE YOU from the bottom of my heart. I stand with you and for you in a bold and courageous way for your restoration and healing, and I will stubbornly never give up on you.

You may be reading this and fortunately have not experienced sexual abuse but are facing other life challenges and struggles that have landed you in a dark, desperate, brokenhearted soul space. I want you to know that I LOVE YOU, as well, and I stand for your healing and restoration, too!

I believe in all of you and your journey in the days, months, and years ahead to reclaim your power back and discover the miracle that you are — your own beautiful, creative, and authentic self! Behind that love for you is a compassion to pour my heart and soul out in the days, years, decades ahead to make sure that you have the opportunity to heal from the devastating impact of any form of abuse—specifically, sexual abuse.

A powerful thing I have discovered about this love and utmost compassion for another is that it truly is the only spark that has the supernatural spiritual power behind it to ignite a new passion inside of you to choose, commit, and want to take action to heal yourself—to create a whole new life for yourself that is centered around a life purpose, strong and unwavering values, and that beautiful leader within that is full of total self-acceptance and authority. For you to stand and give yourself a hug and say that you love your little, teenage, or adult self again as you now have equipped yourself to nurture that wound for the rest of your life. You see, this wound will always have a scar, and behind the scar is the deep heart and soul wounding; however, now in the scar is a restoration to a pure and innocent heart and soul that takes you forward for the rest of your life.

Also, I want to declare something powerful and magical you will soon discover about The Marble Effect:

You are on your way to seeing yourself differently. I have something I want to say to you that comes from this pure heart and soul. You are not just labeled as a victim or survivor of sexual abuse, but you are THRIVING from sexual abuse. You are rising above the abuse with a supernatural, true, spiritual connection that sustains you, now. There is no more abuse of yourself to numb the pain through alcohol, drugs, sex, and any other negative behavior and action that could bring harm on you or others. You are living as the best version of yourself and finding fulfillment and contentment in all areas of your life through a supernatural connection back to all the fruits of the spirit, a true love, peace, and joy. I know this is possible, as I am living it and experiencing the beauty of those supernatural spiritual fruits each day as I continue my healing.

Now, I want you to use your imagination in this beautiful moment. Let me set the stage for you. You have poured out your blood, sweat, and tears over the last several weeks, months, years to confront the darkness, spiritually awaken, continue to heal, and create that pure heart and soul you've always longed for since the trauma. It is now time for you to be seen as the beautiful you, your voice heard loud and clear, and you to be loved for who you are as the naturally resourceful, creative, whole self that you are.

You arrive in this stadium or venue to own and declare your healing. It is now time for you to share your story to inspire hope, inspiration, and transformation. The amazing thing about this is that each one of you is unique and special with your own story to offer humanity.

Now, imagine you are about to walk on stage from the side entrance. All the seats are full of us watching as all our voices take a stand for our lives and rise above the abuse. There is a backdrop of colorful marbles flowing gracefully, peacefully, and freely with a light, subtle, inspirational music tone airing throughout the stadium. The stage floor is completely black, like the darkness that once abounded in your heart and soul. At the center of this stage is a bright, white light shining its rays down on this pure, bright, shiny marble, three-tier, circular platform. Over to the left is a marble chair, where I'm sitting, eagerly awaiting to celebrate, cheer you on, support, and love you along with all the others in the stadium for the courageous, beautiful human being that you are.

There are six steps to walk up to the platform, and as you take that first step, you start to feel those butterflies of excited nervousness, and it's like time freezes as you put one foot in front of the other walking up those steps. As you arrive on the platform, your head is down, and you're staring at that darkness you once lived day in and day out for weeks, months, or years, but now you are confronting it. You realize that you are rising above it with your own wings spread and flying higher. You look up to see that shining podium waiting for you. It's waiting for you to walk up there and claim your own supernatural power and authority, that great-ness within you. As you take a step on the first tier, you feel the moment where your body language and posture has shifted from the darkness of looking down on yourself in defeat, shame, blame, and guilt. You hold your head high, pull your shoulders back in confidence, exuding a warm energy, and keep a smile on your face again, owning and approving your-self as the beautiful you. You slowly walk over to that marble podium where that white, bright light is almost a blinding radiance of purity and innocence.

As you arrive at the steps of the marble podium, you notice all the colorful marbles embedded in risers of the steps. Your pulse is racing as the blood pumps fiercely through your body, and you take the first step being re-minded of that moment of spiritual connection back to Your Creator, that supernatural moment where you feel that light again and are being filled with a zinging spiritual energy. You pause there as you embrace that moment and soak it up. Then, you step up on the second step and are instantly reminded of that magical exploration and discovery of Life Purpose, Values and Leader Within that serves as that foundation to guide you and take you forward for the rest of your life. Finally, the last step brings a forgiving, blissful moment for you as you are acknowledged and championed by us all. The moment to declare what you're once and for all letting go of, what you're choosing for your life, what you're com-mitting to, and what actions you're owning now in this moment to move forward to embrace your most fulfilling, content life. Living life on your terms as the best version of yourself to offer and serve out to the world and others.

You open your mouth and start telling your story. You show up, owning your own power and authority over your life. You give yourself a hug and say, "I LOVE YOU," to yourself. You declare that you are not just a SUR-VIVOR, but a THRIVER from the sexual abuse. As you lean into what you're saying, you're letting go of and saying no, too. You hold a marble up, drop it, and watch it bounce until you choose to stomp it with your foot. You say NO to giving the abuse power over your life. You say no to the darkness, the lies, the manipulation, the deception—all those negative emotions—and most importantly, you say no to abusing yourself physically, emotionally, and spiritually. You're done with that. You let go of whatever it is that had been holding you back. Now, you sit down to play a new game of marbles as you say, yes, each time you flick a marble to knock all the dark marbles off the platform. You say YES to your miraculous, beautiful, authentic self. Say YES to LOVING yourself again, YES to your Life Purpose, Values, and Leader Within. You say YES to continued healing and creating the life that you want. You say YES to being a vessel to support others healing from abuse. Finally, you say YES to FORGIVENESS, not because your abuser deserves it, but because you DESERVE it! The crowd erupts and I run to you to give you a big ol' hug of love, peace, and joy that you so deserve for the rest of your life.

Promise me you will not accept the love from the dark energies, lies, and manipulations of others, but only the love and light from within that connects only with those who share that same light and love, as well.

I want to leave you with some inspirational departing words that I know to be true. I believe and stand for you and your healing to create the life that you want. I believe that you are just as courageous as I am to tell your story and restore purity and innocence back into your heart and soul. I believe that you are special and unique. I believe you only accept the love that you know you deserve in your life. I believe in YOU!

So, that leads me back to the ultimate question, why did I write this book? First and foremost, I wrote it for my next level of healing. Secondly, I wrote this book from a surrendered and vulnerable heart and soul to offer hope, inspiration, and transformation. All I ever wanted to be was the strike of the match that started the fire that has spread among you all, a blazing, raging fire of healing for ourselves. This is not about me, but all

*about us! I'm just one voice to come forward in a supernatural, coura-
geous way to take a stand against silence of abuse. "Silence KILLS!" This
is The Marble Effect movement: it is all of us who want to take back
power over our lives from abuse and share our story to be seen, heard and
loved for who we are and who we are not!*

*I will leave you with this final statement of what it felt like by me not
telling my story for years. "The weight of bearing an untold story within
felt like a brick wall being built on my shoulders each day. Telling my
story has released that weight and set me free. The same is possible for
you, too!" The time is NOW for you to tell your story, not later!*

*As tears of abundance flow freely in this moment of the healing silence
that is present now, I declare that my cup has run over with the deepest
contentment and utmost fulfillment. I am complete for now!*

I love you with all my pure heart and soul!

Paul "Derrick" Hill

Appendix

All rights to Co-Active Coaching Model belong exclusively to:
Co – Active Training Institute
2370 Kerner Blvd, Suite 370
San Rafael, CA 94901
1-800-691-6008
www.coactive.com

Made in the USA
Monee, IL
27 February 2021

61497809R00085